PENGUIN  C

MINOR NOTES,
VOLUME I

JOSHUA BENNETT is a professor of English and creative writing at Dartmouth College. For his creative writing and scholarship, he has received fellowships from the Guggenheim Foundation, the Whiting Foundation, the National Endowment for the Arts, and the Society of Fellows at Harvard University. He is the author of four books of poetry and criticism: *The Sobbing School* (Penguin, 2016), winner of the National Poetry Series; *Being Property Once Myself* (Harvard University Press, 2020), winner of the MLA's William Sanders Scarborough Prize; *Owed* (Penguin, 2020); and *The Study of Human Life* (Penguin, 2022).

JESSE McCARTHY is an assistant professor in the departments of English and of African and African American Studies at Harvard University. His publications include chapter contributions to *Richard Wright in Context, Ralph Ellison in Context,* and *The Cambridge Companion to the Essay,* as well as articles in *Novel, Transposition,* and *African American Review.* He is editor of the 2022 Norton Library edition of W. E. B. Du Bois's *The Souls of Black Folk* and author of *Who Will Pay Reparations on My Soul?,* a collection of essays, and a novel, *The Fugitivities.*

TRACY K. SMITH is the author of the memoir *Ordinary Light,* a finalist for the 2015 National Book Award for Nonfiction, as well as four books of poetry: *Wade in the Water,* winner of the 2019 Anisfield-Wolf Book Award; *Life on Mars,* which received the 2012 Pulitzer Prize; *Duende,* recipient of the 2006 James Laughlin Award; and *The Body's Question,* which won the 2002 Cave Canem Poetry Prize. *Eternity,* her selected poems, was short-listed for the Forward and T. S. Eliot Prizes. Smith served two terms as the twenty-second Poet Laureate Consultant in Poetry of the United States, appointed by the Library of Congress.

Minor Notes,

VOLUME I

Foreword by
TRACY K. SMITH

Edited with an Introduction by
JOSHUA BENNETT *and* JESSE McCARTHY

PENGUIN BOOKS

PENGUIN BOOKS
An imprint of Penguin Random House LLC
penguinrandomhouse.com

LIBRARY OF CONGRESS CATALOGING-IN-PUBLICATION DATA
Names: Smith, Tracy K., writer of foreword. |
Bennett, Joshua (Poet), editor. | McCarthy, Jesse, editor.
Title: Minor notes / foreword by Tracy K. Smith;
edited with an introduction by Joshua Bennett, and Jesse McCarthy.
Description: New York : Penguin Books, [2023] | Includes bibliographical references.
Identifiers: LCCN 2022037769 (print) | LCCN 2022037770 (ebook) |
ISBN 9780143137269 (v. 1 ; paperback) | ISBN 9780593511220 (v. 1 ; ebook)
Subjects: LCSH: American poetry—African American authors. |
African Americans—Poetry. | LCGFT: Poetry.
Classification: LCC PS591.B53 M56 2023 (print) | LCC PS591.B53 (ebook) |
DDC 811.008/0896073—dc23/eng/20220810
LC record available at https://lccn.loc.gov/2022037769
LC ebook record available at https://lccn.loc.gov/2022037770

Printed in the United States of America
1st Printing

Set in Sabon LT Pro

Contents

Foreword by TRACY K. SMITH   xi
Introduction by JOSHUA BENNETT *and*
   JESSE McCARTHY   xv

MINOR NOTES,

VOLUME I

THE POETS

GEORGE MOSES HORTON

Praise of Creation.   3
On the Silence of a Young Lady, On Account
   of the Imaginary Flight of Her Suitor.   5
The Lover's Farewell.   7
On Liberty and Slavery.   8
To Eliza.   10
Love.   11
On the Death of an Infant.   12
The Slave's Complaint.   13
On the Truth of the Saviour.   14
On Spring.   16
On Summer.   18
On Winter.   20
Heavenly Love.   22

On the Death of Rebecca.   23
On Death.   24
On the Evening and Morning.   26
On the Poetic Muse.   28
Consequences of Happy Marriages.   29
Lines, On Hearing of the Intention of a
    Gentleman to Purchase the Poet's Freedom.   31
To the Gad-Fly.   33
The Loss of Female Character.   34

FENTON JOHNSON

Harlem: The Black City.   37
Two Songs.   38
The Creed of the Slave.   40
The Soul of Boston.   41
The Soldiers of the Dusk.   42
Slave Death Song.   43
Jubal's Free.   44
Song of the Whirlwind.   46
My God in Heaven Said to Me.   47
Plantation Sermon.   48
The Phantom Rabbit.   49
S. Coleridge Taylor.   50
Ethiopia.   52
Douglass.   58
Declaration.   60
Comin' Home.   61
The Banjo Player   62
The Scarlet Woman   63
The Minister   64
Rulers: Philadelphia   65
Aunt Hannah Jackson   66
Aunt Jane Allen   67
Tired   68

GEORGIA DOUGLAS JOHNSON

Black Woman   71
Sonnet to Those Who See but Darkly   72
Perspective   73
Cosmopolite   74
Laocoön   75
We Face the Future   76
To Samuel Coleridge Taylor, upon Hearing His
    "Sometimes I Feel Like a Motherless Child"   77
The Measure   78
Shall I Say, "My Son, You're Branded"?   79
Common Dust   80
Old Black Men   81
The Heart of a Woman   82

HENRIETTA CORDELIA RAY

Toussaint L'Ouverture   85
Aspiration.   86
Self-Mastery.   87
Limitations   88
The Poet's Ministrants.   89
Milton.   90
In Memoriam Paul Laurence Dunbar   91
Ode on the Twentieth Century
    (A Dream-Prophecy.)   93

DAVID WADSWORTH CANNON JR.

I. Labor Chants   99
    Black Labor Chant   99
    "Freedom in Mah Soul"   101
II. "Under the Hawthorn Tree"   105
    Old Faithful   105
    Western Town   106

Cheyenne Fiddler 107
Western Plains 108
Canyon Pain 109
Mountains 110
III. "Symbiosis" 111
Boston Tea 111
Resignation 112
Tree Surgery 113
Representation 114
Transfer of Training 115
Heretic 116
Theology 117
Predestination 118
Auntie's Notion 119
Native Intelligence 120
Bank Porter 121
Proof 122
Pok Chops 123
Liberty Bond 124
Economy 125
Ad Infinitum 126
Eclipse 127
Orthodoxy 128
IV. Miscellaneous Poems 129
Pigment 129
To Nita 130
World Weariness—"Weltschmerz" 131

ANNE SPENCER

At the Carnival 135
The Wife-Woman 137
Translation 139
Dunbar 140
[Earth, I Thank You] 141
Grapes: Still-Life 142
Creed 143

Lines to a Nasturtium   144
White Things   145
[God Never Planted a Garden]   146
Life-Long, Poor Browning . . .   147
Questing   148
Before the Feast of Shushan   149
Requiem   151
Change   152
For Jim, Easter Eve   153
Substitution   154
[Thou Art Come to Us, O God, This Year]   155
He Said: 156

ANGELINA WELD GRIMKÉ

Fragment   161
The Black Finger   162
At April   163
Trees   164
A Winter Twilight   165
Tenebris   166
To the Dunbar High School   167
The Eyes of My Regret   168
Death   169
Vigil   170
For the Candle Light   171
Grass Fingers   172
Greenness   173
Brown Girl   174
A Mona Lisa   175
El Beso   176
Oh, My Heart, for the Spring!   177
Under the Days   178
When the Green Lies over the Earth   179

Foreword

In his poem "After Avery R. Young," Pulitzer Prize–winning poet Jericho Brown writes, *The blk mind is a continuous mind.* This line emerges for me as a guiding principle—as a mantra, even—when I consider the work of Black poetry in America, which insists upon the centrality of Black lives to the human story, and offers the terms of memory, music, conscience, and imagination that serve to counteract the many erasures and distortions riddling the prevailing narrative of Black life in this country. Indeed, Black poets help us to consider our past, present, and future not as disparate fragments on a disappearing trail, but rather as a single, emphatic unity: the *Was, Is,* and *Ever-Shall-Be* of Black presence and consciousness.

The blk mind is a continuous mind. And language is one site where the continuum of Black life can be perceived, where we can hear ourselves talking to one another across generations, landscapes, and the particularities of circumstance. Indeed, Black poets also hurl their voices across other types of borders to remind us that we are living, sighing, and singing in harmony with others elsewhere and with traditions beyond our own.

I hear a glimmer of this border-spanning continuity in "Dunbar," Anne Spencer's 1922 homage to the poet Paul Laurence Dunbar:

> Ah, how poets sing and die!
> Make one song and Heaven takes it;
> Have one heart and Beauty breaks it;
> Chatterton, Shelley, Keats and I—
> Ah, how poets sing and die!

In the poem, Spencer, speaking as Dunbar, forgoes the south-
ern Black dialect with which the Black bard is famously asso-
ciated, for which he was frequently criticized, and to which he
sometimes felt uncomfortably obliged. Instead, she aligns him
with the idealism, vulnerability, and uncontested authority of
England's Romantic poets. In fact, Spencer's poem doesn't
bother to argue for Dunbar's ascension to the Western literary
canon; its penultimate line goes so far as to position him firmly
within it. In so doing, perhaps the poem seeks not so much to
liberate Dunbar from the "one song" or "one heart" of his
commitment to Black life, but to remind us that Chatterton,
Shelley, and Keats were, similarly, poets of single-minded
focus and commitment.

   Just as Spencer toggles the frame through which a reader re-
gards Dunbar, *Minor Notes* invites us to listen anew to voices
often occluded by our fixation upon the "headliners" of Afri-
can American poetry. When I do, I am reminded that the con-
versation in which Black poets are currently engaged, in the
turbulent first quarter of the twenty-first century, began gen-
erations and centuries ago when our forebears brought poetic
language to the task of pondering and protesting the elusive
nature of freedom. George Moses Horton's apostrophe to the
elements in "Praise of Creation" includes these lines addressed
to the thunder:

> Responsive thunders roll,
>   Loud acclamations sound,
> And show your Maker's vast control
>   O'er all the worlds around.

Almost two centuries later, Tyehimba Jess's poem "What the
Wind, Rain, and Thunder Said to Tom" seems to meet Hor-
ton's call with a corresponding response, this time addressed
from the elements to mankind:

> Become your own full sky. Own
> every damn sound that struts through your ears.
> Shove notes in your head till they bust out where

your eyes supposed to shine. Cast your lean
brightness across the world and folk will stare

Why is the Black mind a continuous mind? Because the work
of freedom is slow. Therefore, our voices must be ever re-
sourceful, traveling forward and backward in time, lending
themselves to and beyond our own age in an ongoing collec-
tive undertaking.

I like to believe that Gwendolyn Brooks's 1968 poem "The
Second Sermon on the Warpland," in commanding "Live! /
and have your blooming in the noise of the whirlwind," is
seeking in part to tend to and bolster the beleaguered spirit
that calls out from Fenton Johnson's "Song of the Whirlwind":

Oh, my soul is in the whirlwind,
    I am dying in the valley,
Oh, my soul is in the whirlwind
And my bones are in the valley

Angelina Weld Grimké's early 1920s anti-lynching sonnet,
"Trees," seems also to be directly invoked or reactivated by
Brooks's 1957 poem "The *Chicago Defender* Sends a Man to
Little Rock," written to mark the backlash, in Little Rock, Ar-
kansas, against the desegregating presence of the Little Rock
Nine. Grimké's poem closes with the following sestet:

Yet here amid the wistful sounds of leaves,
A black-hued gruesome something swings and swings,
Laughter it knew and joy in little things
Till man's hate ended all. ——And so man weaves.
And God, how slow, how very slow weaves He—
Was Christ Himself not nailèd to a tree?

As if to underscore Grimké's impatience at the slow, slow
weaving of both man and God, Brooks's final lines veer to-
ward the imagery and rhythm of Grimké's—though perhaps
her shortened meter is also an attempt to accelerate the pace of
redress:

I saw a bleeding brownish boy. . . .

The lariat lynch-wish I deplored.

The loveliest lynchee was our Lord.

These and other correspondences between poets and across time periods remind me that Black poetry has long occupied itself with the essential work of stewarding a people—and perhaps *all* people—into the light of freedom. It is a labor of necessity, a struggle under burden. It is also the glorious work of seeding the future.

The blk mind is a continuous mind. Black poets must be awake to their time, attuned to the past, and—in the words of poet and educator David Wadsworth Cannon, who was published only posthumously at the behest of family and friends—ever yearning out toward "the pulse of aeons yet to be."

TRACY K. SMITH

Introduction

The music is in minors.
—GWENDOLYN BROOKS

As scholars of African American literature and cultural history, we repeatedly find ourselves struck by the number of exciting poets we come across in long-out-of-print collections and forgotten journals, whose work has been neglected and, in some cases, entirely ignored, even by those academic circles devoted to its study.

Minor Notes is an excavation initiative that addresses this problem by digging in the crates to recover these understudied, though supremely gifted, African American poets of the nineteenth and twentieth centuries. By pairing selections from historically overlooked collections of poetry with prefatory commentary provided by contemporary poets, our project bridges scholarly interest with the growing audience outside the university that reads, writes, and circulates black poetry. We begin from the premise that the study of black poetry always already takes place in a minor register. We mean this, at present, in at least three distinct ways.

First, we live in a country where poetry in general—though its readership is rising, according to various metrics[1]—remains for the most part ignored by the publishing industry and larger literary world. And although over the past decade black poets living in the United States have begun taking center stage—think here not only of recent Pulitzer Prize winners such as Jericho Brown, Tyehimba Jess, Natasha Trethewey, Gregory

Pardlo, and Tracy K. Smith, who also recently served as poet laureate, but also of two out of the last three inaugural poets: Elizabeth Alexander and Amanda Gorman—it remains our sense that their innovative work is rarely studied as part of a much larger constellation of writers working from a common inheritance; that is, black poets who likewise used their position to challenge dominant genre conventions, create institutional spaces where the imaginations of young people could be nurtured, and offer an unvarnished critique of the life-negating material conditions that millions of our people must navigate each day. With *Minor Notes*, we aim to speak back to any and all atomization of this kind. We aim to clarify that the work of contemporary black poets is perhaps *best* understood through the lens of a longstanding tradition of the poet as witness, as prophetic voice, as communal bard, as scholar of the everyday and the miraculous too.

The second source of our emphasis on *the minor* is that even within the field of black literary studies—itself a small subfield within a historically besieged meta-discipline—there is an enduring aversion at the level of citation, and critical attention more broadly, to *poetry as a genre*. Poetry is quite rarely the focus of dissertations and full-length monographs in our field.[2] This dynamic, we imagine, emerges in part from the much larger cultural problematic already outlined here. Yet this gap, as it pertains to the study of *black poetry in black studies in particular*, remains central enough to our current project that it merits mentioning. The first published black writers in the US context, after all, were poets. Jupiter Hammon and Phillis Wheatley set the stage for each and every one of us, their living descendants: poets, theorists, dreamers, who walk in the light of their shimmering wake. *Minor Notes*, then, as both a series of individual texts and a larger public humanities initiative unfolding beyond the pages of the book you are holding in your hands, seeks to expound upon this historical truth. It will amplify, and echo, the voices of a multitude of black poets who have been undertheorized or altogether ignored. And not just their voices as authors, their unbound stylings on the printed page, but their voices as teachers, community members,

and historical actors; their role in the social and political land-
scapes they helped to shape in their individual contexts.

Third, we intend to celebrate a certain emphasis on *sound*,
on music, on the spoken, that characterizes "the difficult mir-
acle of black poetry in America," as June Jordan once so aptly
put it.[3] Many of the entries contained herein are poems meant
to be read aloud, among the people. These are works penned
by writers who allowed such a black social sensibility, such a
sense of black sociality, to inflect their practice in a way that
continues, even now, to elucidate pathways forward for those
of us presently in search of a liberatory sound. The minor
notes in *Minor Notes* are just that: crawl spaces in the register
where we can more clearly hear what the world calls darkness.
This is listening as a way of reading. What Fred Moten—
drawing from the work of W. E. B. Du Bois and Lindon
Barrett—once called second sight as *audiovision*.[4] A theoreti-
cal practice of attending to the sites and sounds of black social
life within the Veil. Practicing a kind of sustained care for the
full sensory landscape black poetry avails to us.

Our selection process for the authors we have included was
a dynamic one, and it has been ongoing over the past two
years. It began as a conversation at a house party in Jamaica
Plain, Massachusetts. Most of the guests had already left, but
the two of us decided to linger for a bit, and eventually found
ourselves poring over a copy of James Snead's *Figures of Divi-
sion: William Faulkner's Major Novels*. During the course of
our conversation, it became clear that we both had come to
Snead's work through independent study; that we rarely saw
his work cited, though the cultural moment seemed to call out
for his voice. A total original. A stunning collision of theoreti-
cal rigor and rhetorical agility, inordinate elegance holding
fast through and against the stricture of the form. The conver-
sation, quite naturally, moved from critical theory to poetry.
We began to talk about some of our most recent rare finds on-
line, as well as in the used bookstores of Boston and New York
City, scouring the poetry aisle for hidden jewels. A question
eventually settled in the air. It came to guide the rest of our
conversation: Who are, who were, the black minor poets? And

how might we cultivate a method for discerning the minor notes amidst so much noise?

We should say at the outset that our project is only possible because it rests upon a foundation built up primarily by the devoted archivists, scholars, librarians, and bibliophiles who have come before us. Foremost among these is the bibliographer, curator, and librarian Dorothy B. Porter, who produced the first comprehensive bibliographic surveys of early black writing and was the driving force for more than forty years in building up the archives of the Moorland-Spingarn Research Center at Howard University. Porter teamed up with the Afroborinqueño collector and archivist Arturo Alfonso Schomburg to produce *North American Negro Poets: A Bibliographical Checklist of Their Writings, 1760–1944* (published in 1945), an early landmark survey of black poets minor and major alike. Schomburg's *Bibliographical Checklist of American Negro Poetry* (1916) was, in fact, the first bibliography ever devoted specifically to black poets—but his later collaboration with Porter decisively superseded it. Black women have, indeed, often been poet-gatherers and custodians of their own work, as attested, for example, by Gertrude E. H. Bustill Mossell (writing in deference to the gender politics of her time under her husband's name as Mrs. N. F. Mossell), whose *The Work of the Afro-American Woman* (1894) devoted an early essay to "The Afro-American Woman in Verse."

In a list of canonical anthologies assembled by poets, the preeminent pioneer, not least for its remarkable preface, is James Weldon Johnson's *The Book of American Negro Poetry* (1922). Countee Cullen's *Caroling Dusk* (1927) includes deep cuts and classics from the New Negro Renaissance. Scholars and academics active in the first half of the twentieth century, like Vernon Loggins, Benjamin Brawley (himself a minor poet), Arthur P. Davis (coeditor with the poet and scholar Sterling Brown of the classic anthology *The Negro Caravan*, published in 1941), and J. Saunders Redding (author of the important critical study *To Make a Poet Black* [1939]), are, likewise, important anthologizers of early and neglected black writers, including, of course, many poets. In the postwar period, major collections include Langston Hughes and Arna Bontemps's *The Poetry of the Negro, 1746–1949* (1949); Robert Hayden's *Kaleidoscope* (1967); Amiri Baraka and Larry Neal's *Black Fire* (1968), the classic anthology of the Black Arts Movement; Raoul Abdul and Alan Lomax's *3000 Years of Black Poetry* (1970); June Jordan's *Soulscript: Afro-American Poetry* (1970); Jean Wagner's *Black Poets of the United States* (1973); Dudley Randall's *The Black Poets* (1985); and Michael S. Harper and Anthony Walton's *Vintage Book of African American Poetry* (2000). In the new millennium we have Camille T. Dungy's *Black Nature: Four Centuries of African American Nature Poetry* (2009); *Angles of Ascent: A Norton Anthology of Contemporary African American Poetry* (2013), edited by Charles Henry Rowell; *The BreakBeat Poets, Volume 2: Black Girl Magic* (2018), edited by Mahogany L. Browne, Idrissa Simmonds, and Jamila Woods; and, most recently, the epic *African American Poetry: 250 Years of Struggle & Song* (2020), edited by Kevin Young.

Since *Minor Notes* aims to contribute to a history of books devoted specifically to recovering marginalized black poets, we have to make special note of one whose example we draw heavily upon, Joan R. Sherman's *Invisible Poets: Afro-Americans of the Nineteenth Century* (1974). It has now been almost half a century since Sherman's study, and much critical thinking and more recent scholarship have changed how we read and think about black poetics and the history and practice of black literary traditions. Some of the poets we want to draw back into the light appear in these earlier studies. Others do not. But we see our project as changing more than just the content; we want to shift the emphasis and the burden away from proving the existence or validity of black poets to a care for their work premised on the idea that the rich folds tucked away in the tradition are valuable, instructive, and inspiring for their own sake and on their own terms.

Hence, our criteria for inclusion, such as minimal appearances, if any, in popular anthologies and very little, if anything, in the way of secondary literature focusing on their work, ended up being subordinate to a criterion that was a bit more difficult to name at first but that nonetheless became central to our search: the sense of a voice, even one we might be familiar with, so striking it jars you awake. One distinct from what has come before or since. A bridge between where we have been and where we need to get to.

JOSHUA BENNETT *and* JESSE McCARTHY

NOTES

1. See Sunil Iyengar, "Taking Note: Poetry Reading Is Up!— Federal Survey Results," n.d. Retrieved from https://www.arts .gov/stories/blog/2018/taking-note-poetry-reading-federal-survey -results.

2. It is heartening, but telling, in this regard that Ivy G. Wilson's edition *At the Dusk of Dawn: Selected Poetry and Prose of Albery Allson Whitman* (2009) revived the work of a minor poet that had been out of print for nearly a century, including Whitman's *The Rape of Florida* (1884), one of the longest poems by an African American, and one of the few nineteenth-century poems to treat the question of black and indigenous relations and to engage the Seminole Wars from a black writer's perspective.

3. See June Jordan, "The Difficult Miracle of Black Poetry in America or Something Like a Sonnet for Phillis Wheatley," *The Massachusetts Review* 27, no. 2 (1986): 252–62.

4. Fred Moten, *Stolen Life* (Chapel Hill, NC: Duke University Press, 2018), 10.

Minor Notes,

VOLUME I

GEORGE MOSES HORTON

Selections from
Poems by a Slave (1837)

Published in 1837, *Poems by a Slave* is one of the lesser-known works by the writer once popularly known as the "black bard of North Carolina," one George Moses Horton (1798–1883). Over the course of his life, Horton would publish three other collections: *The Hope of Liberty* (1829), *The Poetical Works* (1845), and *Naked Genius* (1865). Despite this remarkable output, Horton's work remains relatively undertheorized in the field of black literary studies.

More than two decades before *Poems by a Slave* was published, Horton began publicly reciting the poems he composed in his head for students on the campus of the University of North Carolina at Chapel Hill. There, as well as at the weekly Chapel Hill farmers market, Horton would sell these invisible works—many of them love poems—to passersby. In addition to purchasing his early work, a number of the students also lent him books. From there, his legend only grew. Eventually, his poems caught the attention of Caroline Lee Whiting Hentz, a novelist who helped transcribe Horton's poems and get them published in a local newspaper.

In 1829, these poems found their way into his debut collection, *The Hope of Liberty*. In 1832, he learned to write. In the

poems and elsewhere, he petitioned for his freedom. Over the
next three decades, Horton would travel with the Ninth Mich-
igan Cavalry Volunteers during the Civil War. He would live
for seventeen years as a free man in Philadelphia before his
death in 1883.

Praise of Creation.

Creation fires my tongue!
  Nature thy anthems raise;
And spread the universal song
  Of thy Creator's praise!

Heaven's chief delight was Man
  Before Creation's birth—
Ordained with joy to lead the van,
  And reign the lord of Earth.

When Sin was quite unknown,
  And all the woes it brought,
He hailed the morn without a groan
  Or one corroding thought.

When each revolving wheel
  Assumed its sphere sublime,
Submissive Earth then heard the peal,
  And struck the march of time.

The march in Heaven begun,
  And splendor filled the skies,
When Wisdom bade the morning Sun
  With joy from chaos rise.

The angels heard the tune
  Throughout creation ring;
They seized their golden harps as soon
  And touched on every string.

When time and space were young,
  And music rolled along—
The morning stars together sung,
  And Heaven was drown'd in song.

Ye towering eagles soar,
 And fan Creation's blaze,
And ye terrific lions roar,
 To your Creator's praise.

Responsive thunders roll,
 Loud acclamations sound,
And show your Maker's vast control
 O'er all the worlds around.

Stupendous mountains smoke,
 And lift your summits high,
To him who all your terrors woke,
 Dark'ning the sapphire sky.

Now let my muse descend,
 To view the march below—
Ye subterraneous worlds attend
 And bid your chorus flow.

Ye vast volcanoes yell
 Whence fiery cliffs are hurled;
And all ye liquid oceans swell
 Beneath the solid world.

Ye cataracts combine,
 Nor let the pæan cease—
The universal concert join,
 Thou dismal precipice.

But halt my feeble tongue,
 My weary muse delays:
But, oh my soul, still float along
 Upon the flood of praise!

On the Silence of a Young Lady,
On account of the imaginary flight of her suitor.

Oh, heartless dove! mount in the skies,
   Spread thy soft wing upon the gale,
Or on thy sacred pinions rise,
   Nor brood with silence in the vale.

Breathe on the air thy plaintive note,
   Which oft has filled the lonesome grove,
And let thy melting ditty float—
   The dirge of long lamented love.

Coo softly to the silent ear,
   And make the floods of grief to roll;
And cause by love the sleeping tear,
   To wake with sorrow from the soul.

Is it the loss of pleasures past
   Which makes thee droop thy sounding wing?
Does winter's rough, inclement blast
   Forbid thy tragic voice to sing?

Is it because the fragrant breeze
   Along the sky forbears to flow—
Nor whispers low amidst the trees,
   Whilst all the vallies frown below?

Why should a frown thy soul alarm,
   And tear thy pleasures from thy breast?
Or veil the smiles of every charm,
   And rob thee of thy peaceful rest.

Perhaps thy sleeping love may wake,
   And hear thy penitential tone;

And suffer not thy heart to break,
  Nor let a princess grieve alone.

Perhaps his pity may return,
  With equal feeling from the heart,
And breast with breast together burn,
  Never—no, never more to part.

Never, till death's resistless blow,
  Whose call the dearest must obey—
In twain together then may go,
  And thus together dwell for aye.

Say to the suitor, Come away,
  Nor break the knot which love has tied—
Nor to the world thy trust betray,
  And fly for ever from thy bride.

The Lover's Farewell.

And wilt thou, love, my soul display,
And all my secret thoughts betray?
I strove, but could not hold thee fast,
My heart flies off with thee at last.

The favorite daughter of the dawn,
On love's mild breeze will soon be gone;
I strove, but could not cease to love,
Nor from my heart the weight remove.

And wilt thou, love, my soul beguile,
And gull thy fav'rite with a smile?
Nay, soft affection answers, nay,
And beauty wings my heart away.

I steal on tiptoe from these bowers,
All spangled with a thousand flowers;
I sigh, yet leave them all behind,
To gain the object of my mind.

And wilt thou, love, command my soul,
And waft me with a light control?—
Adieu to all the blooms of May,
Farewell—I fly with love away!

I leave my parents here behind,
And all my friends—to love resigned—
'Tis grief to go, but death to stay:
Farewell—I'm gone with love away!

On Liberty and Slavery.

Alas! and am I born for this,
    To wear this slavish chain?
Deprived of all created bliss,
    Through hardship, toil and pain!

How long have I in bondage lain,
    And languished to be free!
Alas! and must I still complain—
    Deprived of liberty.

Oh, Heaven! and is there no relief
    This side the silent grave—
To soothe the pain—to quell the grief
    And anguish of a slave?

Come Liberty, thou cheerful sound,
    Roll through my ravished ears!
Come, let my grief in joys be drowned,
    And drive away my fears.

Say unto foul oppression, Cease:
    Ye tyrants rage no more,
And let the joyful trump of peace,
    Now bid the vassal soar.

Soar on the pinions of that dove
    Which long has cooed for thee,
And breathed her notes from Afric's grove,
    The sound of Liberty.

Oh, Liberty! thou golden prize,
    So often sought by blood—
We crave thy sacred sun to rise,
    The gift of nature's God!

Bid Slavery hide her haggard face,
  And barbarism fly:
I scorn to see the sad disgrace
  In which enslaved I lie.

Dear Liberty! upon thy breast,
  I languish to respire;
And like the Swan unto her nest,
  I'd to thy smiles retire.

Oh, blest asylum—heavenly balm!
  Unto thy boughs I flee—
And in thy shades the storm shall calm,
  With songs of Liberty!

To Eliza.

Eliza, tell thy lover why
Or what induced thee to deceive me?
Fare thee well—away I fly—
I shun the lass who thus will grieve me.

Eliza, still thou art my song,
Although by force I may forsake thee;
Fare thee well, for I was wrong
To woo thee while another take thee.

Eliza, pause and think awhile—
Sweet lass! I shall forget thee never:
Fare thee well! although I smile,
I grieve to give thee up for ever.

Eliza, I shall think of thee—
My heart shall ever twine about thee;
Fare thee well—but think of me,
Compell'd to live and die without thee.
"Fare thee well!—and if for ever,
Still for ever fare thee well!"

Love.

Whilst tracing thy visage, I sink in emotion,
   For no other damsel so wond'rous I see;
Thy looks are so pleasing, thy charms so amazing,
   I think of no other, my true-love, but thee.

With heart-burning rapture I gaze on thy beauty,
   And fly like a bird to the boughs of a tree;
Thy looks are so pleasing, thy charms so amazing,
   I fancy no other, my true-love, but thee.

Thus oft in the valley I think, and I wonder
   Why cannot a maid with her lover agree?
Thy looks are so pleasing, thy charms so amazing,
   I pine for no other, my true-love, but thee.

I'd fly from thy frowns with a heart full of sorrow—
   Return, pretty damsel, and smile thou on me;
By every endeavour, I'll try thee for ever,
   And languish until I am fancied by thee.

On the Death of an Infant.

Blest Babe! it at length has withdrawn,
   The Seraphs have rocked it to sleep;
Away with an angelic smile it has gone,
   And left a sad parent to weep!

It soars from the ocean of pain,
   On breezes of precious perfume;
O be not discouraged when death is but gain—
   The triumph of life from the tomb.

With pleasure I thought it my own,
   And smil'd on its infantile charms;
But some mystic bird, like an eagle, came down,
   And snatch'd it away from my arms.

Blest Babe, it ascends into Heaven,
   It mounts with delight at the call;
And flies to the bosom from whence it was given,
   The Parent and Patron of all.

The Slave's Complaint.

Am I sadly cast aside,
On misfortune's rugged tide?
Will the world my pains deride
        For ever?

Must I dwell in Slavery's night,
And all pleasure take its flight,
Far beyond my feeble sight,
        For ever?

Worst of all, must Hope grow dim,
And withhold her cheering beam?
Rather let me sleep and dream
        For ever!

Something still my heart surveys,
Groping through this dreary maze;
Is it Hope?—then burn and blaze
        For ever!

Leave me not a wretch confined,
Altogether lame and blind—
Unto gross despair consigned,
        For ever!

Heaven! in whom can I confide?
Canst thou not for all provide?
Condescend to be my guide
        For ever:

And when this transient life shall end,
Oh, may some kind, eternal friend
Bid me from servitude ascend,
        For ever!

On the Truth of the Saviour.

E'en John the Baptist did not know
   Who Christ the Lord could be,
And bade his own disciples go,
   The strange event to see.

They said, Art thou the one of whom
   'Twas written long before?
Is there another still to come,
   Who will all things restore?

This is enough, without a name—
   Go, tell him what is done;
Behold the feeble, weak and lame,
   With strength rise up and run.

This is enough—the blind now see,
   The dumb Hosannas sing;
Devils far from his presence flee,
   As shades from morning's wing.

See the distress'd, all bathed in tears,
   Prostrate before him fall;
Immanuel speaks, and Lazarus hears—
   The dead obeys his call.

This is enough—the fig-tree dies,
   And withers at his frown;
Nature her God must recognise,
   And drop her flowery crown.

At his command the fish increase,
   And loaves of barley swell—
Ye hungry eat, and hold your peace,
   And find a remnant still.

At his command the water blushed,
   And all was turned to wine,
And in redundance flowed afresh,
   And owned its God divine.

Behold the storms at his rebuke,
   All calm upon the sea—
How can we for another look,
   When none can work as he?

This is enough—it must be God,
   From whom the plagues are driven;
At whose command the mountains nod
   And all the Host of Heaven!

On Spring.

Hail, thou auspicious vernal dawn!
Ye birds, proclaim the winter's gone,
    Ye warbling minstrels sing;
Pour forth your tribute as ye rise,
And thus salute the fragrant skies
      The pleasing smiles of Spring.

Coo sweetly, oh thou harmless Dove,
And bid thy mate no longer rove,
    In cold, hybernal vales;
Let music rise from every tongue,
Whilst winter flies before the song,
      Which floats on gentle gales.

Ye frozen streams dissolve and flow
Along the valley, sweet and slow;
    Divested fields be gay;
Ye drooping forests bloom on high,
And raise your branches to the sky,
      And thus your charms display.

Thou world of heat—thou vital source,
The torpid insects feel thy force,
    Which all with life supplies;
Gardens and orchards richly bloom,
And send a gale of sweet perfume,
      To invite them as they rise.

Near where the crystal waters glide,
The male of birds escorts his bride,
    And twitters on the spray;
He mounts upon his active wing,
To hail the bounty of the Spring,
      The lavish pomp of May.

Inspiring month of youthful Love,
How oft we in the peaceful grove,
    Survey the flowery plume;
Or sit beneath the sylvan shade,
Where branches wave above the head,
    And smile on every bloom.

Exalted month, when thou art gone,
May Virtue then begin the dawn
    Of an eternal Spring?
May raptures kindle on my tongue,
And start a new, eternal song,
    Which ne'er shall cease to ring!

On Summer.

Esteville fire begins to burn;
   The auburn fields of harvest rise;
The torrid flames again return,
   And thunders roll along the skies.

Perspiring Cancer lifts his head,
   And roars terrific from on high;
Whose voice the timid creatures dread,
   From which they strive with awe to fly.

The night-hawk ventures from his cell,
   And starts his note in evening air;
He feels the heat his bosom swell,
   Which drives away the gloom of fear.

Thou noisy insect, start thy drum;
   Rise lamp-like bugs to light the train;
And bid sweet Philomela come,
   And sound in front the nightly strain.

The bee begins her ceaseless hum,
   And doth with sweet exertions rise;
And with delight she stores her comb,
   And well her rising stock supplies.

Let sportive children well beware,
   While sprightly frisking o'er the green;
And carefully avoid the snare,
   Which lurks beneath the smiling scene.

The mistress bird assumes her nest,
   And broods in silence on the tree,
Her note to cease, her wings at rest,
   She patient waits her young to see.

The farmer hastens from the heat;
  The weary plough-horse droops his head;
The cattle all at noon retreat,
  And ruminate beneath the shade.

The burdened ox with dauntless rage,
  Flies heedless to the liquid flood,
From which he quaffs, devoid of gauge,
  Regardless of his driver's rod.

Pomaceous orchards now expand
  Their laden branches o'er the lea;
And with their bounty fill the land,
  While plenty smiles on every tree.

On fertile borders, near the stream,
  Now gaze with pleasure and delight;
See loaded vines with melons teem—
  'Tis paradise to human sight.

With rapture view the smiling fields,
  Adorn the mountain and the plain,
Each, on the eve of Autumn, yields
  A large supply of golden grain.

On Winter.

When smiling Summer's charms are past,
    The voice of music dies;
Then Winter pours his chilling blast
    From rough inclement skies.

The pensive dove shuts up her throat,
    The larks forbear to soar,
Or raise one sweet, delightful note,
    Which charm'd the ear before.

The screech-owl peals her shivering tone
    Upon the brink of night;
As some sequestered child unknown,
    Which feared to come in sight.

The cattle all desert the field,
    And eager seek the glades
Of naked trees, which once did yield
    Their sweet and pleasant shades.

The humming insects all are still,
    The beetles rise no more,
The constant tinkling of the bell,
    Along the heath is o'er.

Stern Boreas hurls each piercing gale
    With snow-clad wings along,
Discharging volleys mixed with hail
    Which chill the breeze of song.

Lo, all the Southern windows close,
    Whence spicy breezes roll;
The herbage sinks in sad repose,
    And Winter sweeps the whole.

Thus after youth old age comes on,
    And brings the frost of time,
And e'er our vigour has withdrawn,
    We shed the rose of prime.

Alas! how quick it is the case,
    The scion youth is grown—
How soon it runs its morning race,
    And beauty's sun goes down.

The Autumn of declining years
    Must blanch the father's head,
Encumbered with a load of cares,
    When youthful charms have fled.

Heavenly Love.

Eternal spring of boundless grace,
    It lifts the soul above,
Where God the Son unveils his face,
    And shows that Heaven is love.

Love that revolves through endless years—
    Love that can never pall;
Love which excludes the gloom of fears,
    Love to whom God is all!

Love which can ransom every slave,
    And set the pris'ner free;
Gild the dark horrors of the grave,
    And still the raging sea.

Let but the partial smile of Heaven
    Upon the bosom play,
The mystic sound of sins forgiven,
    Can waft the soul away.

The pilgrim's spirits show this love,
    They often soar on high;
Languish from this dim earth to move,
    And leave the flesh to die.

Sing, oh my soul, rise up and run,
    And leave this clay behind;
Wing thy swift flight beyond the sun,
    Nor dwell in tents confined.

On the Death of Rebecca.

Thou delicate blossom! thy short race is ended,
    Thou sample of virtue and prize of the brave!
No more are thy beauties by mortals attended,
    They now are but food for the worms and the grave.

Thou art gone to the tomb, whence there's no returning,
    And left us behind in a vale of suspense;
In vain to the dust do we follow thee mourning,
    The same doleful trump will soon call us all hence.

I view thee now launched on eternity's ocean,
    Thy soul how it smiles as it floats on the wave;
It smiles as if filled with the softest emotion,
    But looks not behind on the frowns of the grave.

The messenger came from afar to relieve thee—
    In this lonesome valley no more shalt thou roam;
Bright seraphs now stand on the banks to receive thee,
    And cry, "Happy stranger, thou art welcome at home."

Thou art gone to a feast, while thy friends are bewailing,
    Oh, death is a song to the poor ransom'd slave;
Away with bright visions the spirit goes sailing,
    And leaves the frail body to rest in the grave.

Rebecca is free from the pains of oppression,
    No friends could prevail with her longer to stay;
She smiles on the fields of eternal fruition,
    Whilst death like a bridegroom attends her away.

She is gone in the whirlwind—ye seraphs attend her,
    Through Jordan's cold torrent her mantle may lave;
She soars in the chariot, and earth falls beneath her,
    Resign'd in a shroud to a peaceable grave.

On Death.

Deceitful worm, that undermines the clay,
Which slyly steals the thoughtless soul away,
Pervading neighborhoods with sad surprise,
Like sudden storms of wind and thunder rise.

The sounding death-watch lurks within the wall,
Away some unsuspecting soul to call;
The pendant willow droops her waving head,
And sighing zephyrs whisper of the dead.

Methinks I hear the doleful midnight knell—
Some parting spirit bids the world farewell;
The taper burns as conscious of distress,
And seems to show the living number less.

Must a lov'd daughter from her father part,
And grieve for one who lies so near her heart?
And must she for the fatal loss bemoan,
Or faint to hear his last departing groan.

Methinks I see him speechless gaze awhile,
And on her drop his last paternal smile;
With gushing tears closing his humid eyes,
The last pulse beats, and in her arms he dies.

With pallid cheeks she lingers round his bier,
And heaves a farewell sigh with every tear;
With sorrow she consigns him to the dust,
And silent owns the fatal sentence just.

Still her sequestered mother seems to weep,
And spurns the balm which constitutes her sleep;
Her plaintive murmurs float upon the gale,
And almost make the stubborn rocks bewail.

O what is like the awful breach of death,
Whose fatal stroke invades the creature's breath!
It bids the voice of desolation roll,
And strikes the deepest awe within the bravest soul.

On the Evening and Morning.

When Evening bids the Sun to rest retire,
Unwearied Ether sets her lamps on fire;
Lit by one torch, each is supplied in turn,
Till all the candles in the concave burn.

The night-hawk now, with his nocturnal tone,
Wakes up, and all the Owls begin to moan,
Or heave from dreary vales their dismal song,
Whilst in the air the meteors play along.

At length the silver queen begins to rise,
And spread her glowing mantle in the skies,
And from the smiling chambers of the east,
Invites the eye to her resplendent feast.

What joy is this unto the rustic swain,
Who from the mount surveys the moon-lit plain;
Who with the spirit of a dauntless *Pan*
Controls his fleecy train and leads the van;

Or pensive, muses on the water's side,
Which purling doth thro' green meanders glide,
With watchful care he broods his heart away
'Till night is swallowed in the flood of day.

The meteors cease to play, that mov'd so fleet
And spectres from the murky groves retreat,
The prowling wolf withdraws, which howl'd so bold
And bleating flocks may venture from the fold.

The night-hawk's din deserts the shepherd's ear.
Succeeded by the huntsman's trumpet clear,
O come Diana, start the morning chase
Thou ancient goddess of the hunting race.

Aurora's smiles adorn the mountain's brow,
The peasant hums delighted at his plough,
And lo, the dairy maid salutes her bounteous cow.

On the Poetic Muse.

Far, far above this world I soar,
    And almost nature lose,
Aerial regions to explore,
    With this ambitious Muse.

My towering thoughts with pinions rise,
    Upon the gales of song,
Which waft me through the mental skies,
    With music on my tongue.

My Muse is all on mystic fire,
    Which kindles in my breast;
To scenes remote she doth aspire,
    As never yet exprest.

Wrapt in the dust she scorns to lie,
    Call'd by new charms away;
Nor will she e'er refuse to try
    Such wonders to survey.

Such is the quiet bliss of soul,
    When in some calm retreat,
Where pensive thoughts like streamlets roll,
    And render silence sweet;

And when the vain tumultuous crowd
    Shakes comfort from my mind,
My Muse ascends above the cloud
    And leaves the noise behind.

With vivid flight she mounts on high
    Above the dusky maze,
And with a perspicacious eye
    Doth far 'bove nature gaze.

Consequences of Happy Marriages.

Hail happy pair, from whom such raptures rise,
On whom I gaze with pleasure and surprise;
From thy bright rays the gloom of strife is driven,
For all the smiles of mutual love are Heaven.

Thrice happy pair! no earthly joys excel
Thy peaceful state; there constant pleasures dwell,
Which cheer the mind and elevate the soul,
Whilst discord sinks beneath their soft control.

The blaze of zeal extends from breast to breast,
While Heaven supplies each innocent request;
And lo! what fond regard their smiles reveal,
Attractive as the magnet to the steel.

Their peaceful life is all content and ease,
They with delight each other strive to please;
Each other's charms, *they* only can admire,
Whose bosoms burn with pure connubial fire.

Th' indelible vestige of unblemished love,
Must hence a guide to generations prove:
Though virtuous partners moulder in the tomb,
Their light may shine on ages yet to come.

With grateful tears their well-spent day shall close,
When death, like evening, calls them to repose;
Then mystic smiles may break from deep disguise,
Like Vesper's torch transpiring in the skies.

Like constellations still their works may shine,
In virtue's unextinguished blaze divine;
Happy are they whose race shall end the same—
Sweeter than odours is a virtuous name.

Such is the transcript of unfading grace,
Reflecting lustre on a future race,
The virtuous on this line delight to tread,
And magnify the honors of the dead—

Who like a Phoenix did not burn in vain,
Incinerated to revive again;
From whose exalted urn young love shall rise,
Exulting from a funeral sacrifice.

Lines,

On hearing of the intention of a gentleman to purchase the Poet's freedom.

When on life's ocean first I spread my sail,
I then implored a mild auspicious gale;
And from the slippery strand I took my flight,
And sought the peaceful haven of delight.

Tyrannic storms arose upon my soul,
And dreadful did their mad'ning thunders roll;
The pensive muse was shaken from her sphere,
And hope, it vanish'd in the clouds of fear.

At length a golden sun broke through the gloom,
And from his smiles arose a sweet perfume—
A calm ensued, and birds began to sing,
And lo! the sacred muse resumed her wing.

With frantic joy she chaunted as she flew,
And kiss'd the clement hand that bore her through;
Her envious foes did from her sight retreat,
Or prostrate fall beneath her burning feet.

'Twas like a proselyte, allied to Heaven—
Or rising spirits' boast of sins forgiven,
Whose shout dissolves the adamant away,
Whose melting voice the stubborn rocks obey.

'Twas like the salutation of the dove,
Borne on the zephyr through some lonesome grove,
When Spring returns, and Winter's chill is past,
And vegetation smiles above the blast.

'Twas like the evening of a nuptial pair,
When love pervades the hour of sad despair—
'Twas like fair Helen's sweet return to Troy,
When every Grecian bosom swell'd with joy.

The silent harp which on the osiers hung,
Was then attuned, and manumission sung:
Away by hope the clouds of fear were driven,
And music breathed my gratitude to Heaven.

Hard was the race to reach the distant goal,
The needle oft was shaken from the pole;
In such distress who could forbear to weep?
Toss'd by the headlong billows of the deep!

The tantalizing beams which shone so plain,
Which turned my former pleasures into pain—
Which falsely promised all the joys of fame,
Gave way, and to a more substantial flame.

Some philanthropic souls as from afar,
With pity strove to break the slavish bar;
To whom my floods of gratitude shall roll,
And yield with pleasure to their soft control.

And sure of Providence this work begun—
He shod my feet this rugged race to run;
And in despite of all the swelling tide,
Along the dismal path will prove my guide.

Thus on the dusky verge of deep despair,
Eternal Providence was with me there;
When pleasure seemed to fade on life's gay dawn,
And the last beam of hope was almost gone.

To the Gad-Fly.

Majestic insect! from thy royal hum,
The flies retreat, or starve before they'll come;
The obedient plough-horse may, devoid of fear,
Perform his task with joy, when thou art near.

As at the Lion's dread alarming roar,
The inferior beasts will never wander more,
Lest unawares he should be seized away,
And to the prowling monster fall a prey.

With silent pleasure often do I trace
The fly upon the wing, with rapid pace,
The fugitive proclaims upon the wind,
The death-bound sheriff is not far behind.

Ye thirsty flies beware, nor dare approach,
Nor on the toiling animal encroach;
Be vigilant, before you buzz too late,
The victim of a melancholy fate.

Such seems the caution of the once chased fly,
Whilst to the horse she dare not venture nigh;
This useful Gad-Fly traversing the field,
With care the lab'ring animal to shield.

Such is the eye of Providential care,
Along the path of life forever there;
Whose guardian hand by day doth mortals keep
And gently lays them down at night to sleep.

Immortal Guard, shall I thy pleasures grieve
Like Noah's dove, wilt thou the creature leave;
No never, never, whilst on earth I stay,
And after death, then fly with me away.

The Loss of Female Character.

See that fallen Princess! her splendor is gone—
The pomp of her morning is over;
Her day-star of pleasure refuses to dawn,
She wanders a nocturnal rover.

Alas! she resembles Jerusalem's fall,
The fate of that wonderful city;
When grief with astonishment rung from the wall,
Instead of the heart cheering ditty.

When music was silent, no more to be rung,
When Sion wept over her daughter;
On grief's drooping willow their harps they were hung,
When pendent o'er Babylon's water.

She looks like some Star that has fall'n from her sphere,
No more by her cluster surrounded;
Her comrades of pleasure refuse her to cheer,
And leave her dethron'd and confounded.

She looks like some Queen who has boasted in vain,
Whose diamond refuses to glitter;
Deserted by those who once bow'd in her train,
Whose flight to her soul must be bitter.

She looks like the twilight, her sun sunk away,
He sets; but to rise again never!
Like the Eve, with a blush bids farewell to the day,
And darkness conceals her forever.

FENTON JOHNSON

Selections from *Visions of the Dusk* (1915)

In his 1987 book of essays, *The New Sentence*, Ron Silliman narrates the history of the prose poem in English through a poet whose earliest work received mixed reviews to that point—James Weldon Johnson once wrote that the young writer's debut collection, *A Little Dreaming*, "was without marked distinction"—but clearly left a formal mark that, from his vantage, demanded rigorous engagement. Silliman writes: "[Fenton] Johnson uses a device which points in the direction of the new sentence. Each sentence is a complete paragraph; run-on sentences are treated as one paragraph each, but two paragraphs begin with conjunctions. Structured thus, Johnson's is the first American prose poem with a clear, if simple, sentence: paragraph relation."

On the basis of this level of formal innovation alone, one imagines that the impact of Fenton Johnson (1888–1958) within the field of American literary studies would be much more widely felt. Yet there is remarkably little critical attention paid to his work. Born to a middle-class black family in Chicago, he spent much of his childhood there, and eventually pursued undergraduate and graduate degrees at Northwestern University, the University of Chicago, and the Pulitzer School of Journalism at Columbia. After finishing his formal education, he taught as a professor at the historically black State University at Louisville, and eventually worked as a journalist for the *New York News* and the Eastern Press Association before helping to cofound two publications: the *Champion* and the *Favorite*.

By the end of his life, Johnson would self-publish three collections: *A Little Dreaming* (1913), *Visions of the Dusk* (1915), and *Songs of the Soil* (1916). An unpublished fiction manuscript, *A Wild Plaint*, was discovered in 2017.

Harlem: The Black City.

I.

We live and die, and what we reap
Is merely chaff from life's storehouse;
For devil's grain we barter souls
And in his wine our bodies souse;
We build to Pleasure monuments;
But Pleasure always passes by.
The grave!—The grave! our only hope,
The grave where dust grimed failures lie.

II.

We ask for life, men give us wine,
We ask for rest, men give us death;
We long for Pan and Phoebus harp.
But Bacchus blows on us his breath.
O Harlem, weary are thy sons
Of living that they never chose;
Give not to them the lotus leaf,
But Mary's wreath and England's rose.

Two Songs.

I.
The Song of the Passing.

1.

I am weary of this loving and this grieving,
Lay me down beneath the bending willows,
Strew upon me petals of the bleeding roses,
    O my mourners.

2.

I am weary of this loving and this sighing,
Bring me sweet Hallelujah ere I meet the boatman
By the shining waters of the mystic river,
    O my mourners.

3.

Let me hear the breezes singing low of Heaven,
Let me feel the cool of earth upon my body,
Let me hear the laughter of the little children,
    O my mourners.

II.
The Song of the Dusk*

1.
I am the dusk,
The dreamborn soul
    Of yesterday;
I am the hope
Of true Love's birth,—
    The Man in Chains.

2.
I am the star
Whose light descends
    Beneath the sea;
I am the rose
Whose perfume lives
    Beyond the years.

3.
I am thy rod,
I am thy staff,
    O brothers pale;
For thee I live,
For thee I die,
    O brothers mine.

*A title for this section in the original manuscript is missing, but there is strong reason to believe Johnson would have intended for it to mirror the previous title and address the subject of the dusk, hence "The Song of the Dusk."

The Creed of the Slave.

1.

Ah lubs de worl'.—Kain't he'p it, dat's mah way.
Futh'mo' Ah lubs de night, Ah lubs de day,
Ah lubs de suff'rin' crittuhs dat Gawd made,
De li'l 'uns playin' 'neaf de locus' shade,
Ah lubs de shadduhs by de gret big road,
Ah lubs to tote wid me de hebby load
Thoo'all de live long night an' thoo' de day.
Ah lubs de worl'.—Kain't he'p it, dat's mah way.

2.

Go crack yo' whups, an' break dis flesh o' mine,
Ah ain't a-gwine tuh, leave dis love behin';
Ah wu'k an' bleed fu' dose dat hu't me mos',
But in de mawnin' w'en Ah am a ghos'
Ah pray de Lawd dat you kin come up daih
An' play wid me erpon de golden staih.
Ah lubs you all, po' suff'rin' clay;—
Ah lubs de worl'.—Kain't he'p it, dat's mah way.

The Soul of Boston.

My cobblestones are red with England's blood,
My parks are monuments of other days,
My battle cry the cry that right is might,
Humanity my God and mother love.
I blush when Justice cowers in the dust,
When once again we lead to Calvary
The Nazarene enwrapt in scarlet cloak.
I am the sister of the man oppressed,
The sword that flashed at primal Eden's gate,
"No man may enter save the pure in heart."
I sit at Plato's feet, and glean the gold
That drifts from such a rich eternal mind;
Good England's culture is my fading past,
Columbia the glory of my dreams.
O sisters mine, go sound your drums of gold,
Go build your monuments to Greed and Pelf,
For I would rather cherish martyrs' blood
Than all the wealth enshrined in Amsterdam,
And I would rather boast the motherhood
Of Attucks and of Shaw than rule the world.
O God of Winthrop, here I spread Thy couch,
For I have kept Thy faith despite the age.

The Soldiers of the Dusk.

I.

Black men holding up the earth,
Atlas burdened they descend
Deep into the vale of Hell;
And with valor long defend
Fairer brothers from the wounds
That the dogs of war inflict,
And with patriotic souls
Die in Europe's last conflict.

II.

Paris shall not fall so long
As there breathes a man of dusk,
London shall be saved an age
By the fighters of the dusk;
Zulu, robbed of land and home,
For the robber bares his heart,
Kaffir, giving Europe gems,
Europe pierces with a dart.

III.

They are pagan, men of blood,
They have not a golden rule,
Cannibals and fetish men
With their laws intensely cruel;
But the God of Calvary
Will in years unborn be just
To the men who died for men,
Victims of the war god's lust.

Slave Death Song.

1.

Oh, my chariot is swinging,
  Jesus, bring it near,
Soft I hear the harp a-ringing,
  Jesus, bring it near,
All my troubles are a-dying,
Low within the grave a-lying,
Angels o'er my bones a-bending,
Peace and rest to me descending;
  Jesus, bring it near.

2.

Throne of God is shining brightly,
  Jesus, bring it near,
Angels stepping round it sprightly,
  Jesus, take me home.
Curved coach with jasper cover
Swinging for the dusky lover;
White robed choir is sweetly singing,
Glory music earthward bringing,
  Jesus, take me home.

3.

Scythe of Heaven gently reaping,
  Jesus, bring it near,
Love eternal o'er me creeping,
  Jesus, bring it near;
Day within the West is dying,
O'er me summer breeze is sighing,
  To my mother's breast returning,
  For me long she has been yearning;
  Jesus, take me home.

Jubal's Free.

1.

Sound the trumpet, honey,
  Jubal's free,
Sound the ram horn, honey,
  Jubal's free;
Devil goes a-quaking,
Mighty Hell is shaking,
All the stars are tumbling,
Heaven's thunder rumbling,
  Jubal's free.

2.

Dance the Gospel, honey,
  Jubal's free,
Set your feet a-swinging,
  Jubal's free;
Night has changed to morning,
In her breast the warning
Of the God of sorrow,
"They must go to-morrow,"
  Jubal's free.

3.

Ring the church bells, honey,
  Jubal's free;
Set the chimes a-pealing,
  Jubal's free;
God above is shouting,
Devil goes a-pouting,
Earth and sky is meeting,
Freedom is their greeting,
  Jubal's free.

4.

Shake the hand, my brother,
    Jubal's free,
Sing your loudest, brother,
    Jubal's free;
Toss your head to Heaven,
Living's like the leaven,
Earth is rich with sunlight,
Night is rich with moonlight,
    Jubal's free.

Song of the Whirlwind.

1.

Oh, my God is in the whirlwind,
    I am walking in the valley;
Lift me up, O Shining Father,
To the glory of the heavens,
I have seen a thousand troubles
On the journey men call living,
I have drunk a thousand goblets
From misfortune's bitter winepress,
But to Thee I cling forever,
God of Jacob, God of Rachel.

2.

Oh, my soul is in the whirlwind,
    I am dying in the valley,
Oh, my soul is in the whirlwind
And my bones are in the valley;
At her spinning wheel is Mary
Spinning raiment of the lillies,
On her knees is Martha honey
Shining bright the golden pavement,
All the ninety nine is waiting
For my coming, for my coming.

My God in Heaven Said to Me.

1.

My God in Heaven said to me,
"Your mansion's ready in the sky,
Come home, my weary wanderer,
And eat with Me the bread of life,
For I have slain the fatted calf,
For I have filled the honey bowl
And thou shalt always dwell with me.
Come home, my weary wanderer,"
My God in Heaven said to me.

2.

And now I board the Gospel train,
For I am going home to-night
To meet my God on Jordan's coast.
My burdens to the wind I toss,
To-morrow freedom shall be mine;—
A golden crown with burning stars,
And harp of David in my hand
That I may chant the Gospel tunes.

3.

On God's plantation I shall dwell,
The overseer of happiness,
And dance with Israel the dance
Of holiness and righteousness,
A thousand years with God to dwell
Is like a holiday below;
And Oh, my heart was glad to hear
My God in Heaven say to me,
"Your mansion's ready in the sky."

Plantation Sermon.

Doan' you hyeah me preachin',
    Chillun in de valley?
Doan' you hyeah me 'spoundin',
    Chillun in de valley?
Freedom sh's a comin'
In de Savior's keeridge,
Ah kin hyeah it shoutin'
F'um de mouf ob cannons;
Oh, de robes am whituh
Dan de light ob mawnin'
Oh, de songs am sweetuh
Dan de banjo's tummin',
Mighty am de gethrin'
Ob de wounded chillun,
Mighty am de buhstin'
F'um de th'oats ob singuhs.
Git yo' clo's a-ready,
Cleah yo' cotton patches,
Set yo' feet a-dancin'
In de Gospel mannah,
Ah kin hyeah de blowin'
Ob de golden trumpets.
Freedom's hitched huh hosses
An' she's drawin' nighuh.
Bury all yo' troubles,
Bury all yo' grievin's,
God hab hyeahed yo' prayin'—
Freedom's in de whirlwind,
An' we's in de valley.

The Phantom Rabbit.

1.

Look, my weary brother, ere you die;
Night is here, and phantom nigh;
Soul of rabbit with the magic breath,
Soul of Life and foe of living Death.
    Ere we die, my brother, ere we die.

2.

Look, my weary sister, ere we die;
O'er the hills the phantom shadows lie;
Rabbit ghostly soothes your aching fears,
Rabbit ghostly dries your endless tears,
    Ere we die, my sister, ere we die.

S. Coleridge Taylor.

1.

Mute thy strings, O Israfel:
Quenched thy fire, and shrouded low
Men who marvelled at the spell
And the weird but dream borne glow
 Of thy master song.

2.

Israfel, no singers rise
Who can lift thy laurel crown,
Thou alone to glory rise—
Star of England's fair renown
 And the dusk man's hope.

3.

When the Master came thou heard
Music woven of the night,
And, as soars a fleet winged bird,
Thou in melody made flight
 To the Throne of God.

4.

Will the meadows bloom again?
Will the lark in passion song
Lead us to his leafy den?
Will the day remain as long?
 Israfel has gone.

5.
Live to sing as he has sung,
Live to know the heart of God,
Live to speak an angel tongue
And to kiss the moistened sod
O'er our Israfel.

Ethiopia.

O minstrel lyre of ancient Ethiop,
Whose flaming song awoke the Orient,
O long forgotten harp, whose mouldering strings
Hath once enthralled the hearts of warriors,
I pray thee let my burning fingers press
Thee once again that I may sing my song
Ere from my veins the warmth of life hath flown.
O minstrel lyre, no longer do the kings
On couch of leopard skins await thy hour;
The Gods are dead, our ancient glory dust,
Our altars broken, and our people gone,—
Gone whence men quaff the wine of melting pot.
O Libya, for thee the Prophet longs,
O Egypt, born of Sphinx and shadow forms,
O Ethiop, the flame of desert sands,
Thy hour! Thy hour! Oh, when shall come thy hour?

I touch the ancient lyre, and burning sing
The song of Ethiopia the Queen,
The song of her who sits among the gates,
Her eye upon the dawn of liberty and hope.

I.

The groves of Libya with perfume droop,
The dancing maidens, born of dusk and dew,
Before the flame their weirdest chants have raised,
The moon that lives for love and love alone
From vale within the sky beholds the earth;
On throne of cedar, ophyr, and of gold
The jewelled monarch sits, a man of dusk,
Too opulent of war and cruelty,
Too drunk with power, too weak for noble deeds,
His star the strength that lives in mighty arms,
That sweeps before it all the tribes of earth,

He is the morning of the human race,
The first sweet cup of wine existence drinks,
And on the altar luxury he falls,
A broken goblet in the hands of Time.
(Of such has been the human chronicle,
The Caesars, Ptolemies, Alexanders fall,
Great Pompey is the dust of long ago,
And star swept Bonaparte hath met his doom.)
Behind a Northern Chariot the king
With chains of gold around his ebon neck
Must grace the triumph of his enemy,
His people must in slavery bend low,—
The moon of love hath died within the East.
A stranger walks within the grove enow;
But in the years to come that stranger falls
Before another.—So the will of God
Removes the nations, races, and the tribes,
Lest man should be the peer of God Himself.

II.

I hear the martial beat of long ago,
The clash of steel, the tread of Persian hordes.
O Ethiop, how desolate thy shores!
How deep into oblivion thy star!
Thy children's children shall forget thy name,
Forget thy altars, and thy sacred fires,
For from the parching sands of Araby,
Mohammed rides with death or Allah's law.
The wandering tribes of Abyssinia,—
From whence the Sheban queen her journey made,—
Alone survive the glory of the past,
But not the mandates of our ancient gods.
The haughty race that built the pyramids,
That chained the lion and the leopard cub,
With bleeding wounds are prostrate to the West;
In bondage to the priest of Christ and love
Exiled the men of dusk must dwell a day.
The pale and yellow haired from distant shores

Rob Ghana of her bronze and Congo land
Yields tortured slaves to grace a Christian age.
O, World Anew, from splendours barbaric,
From fields of cocoa and of drooping date,
From houses built of sunkist bamboo straw
Thou bringest fathers of a newer race,
Their wrists engyved, their souls in bitterness.
O Mighty Universal Deity,
Upon these exiles pour thy wond'rous love,
For sorrow shall be theirs and loneliness
Among a people who forget the name
Of star crowned Ethiop and Nubia.

III.

The chains that man hath forged the heavens break,
Divine is liberty the slaves achieve;
And Hayti smoulders with the flames of dusk,
Her saviour loving Toussaint, prince of men.
The years may glide beyond the tide of time,
The stars may dim with age, and life grow faint,
But all the sons of men shall not forget
The Western Nazarene who died with love
For those whose treachery caused his death.
O Toussaint, may thy grave be ever green
With wreaths from all oppressed throughout the world,
May fifty thousand drums reveille roll,
A tribute to thy precious memory.
With thee the renaissance of Ethiop
Achieved, like other fires, was quenched awhile;
The cruel splendour Christophe embraced,
The anarchy that followed Citadels
Was not of thee, or thine, great Star of Dusk.
Thy message came to old Virginia's woods,
"Ah! Freemen shall we be," gaunt Turner cries,
And with the courage of the patriot
He fought a day to give our land the glow
Of liberty, fraternity, and love.
He fought a day, and died a traitor's death,

But bright his halo, green his laurel crown.
Each blow for freedom struck is freedom's gain,
And Ethiop shall yet stretch forth her hand.

IV.

When Night surrounds the slave, and hope lies cold,
The daytime breaks and Frederic is borne
On Fortune's tide to plead the cause of right.
Men marvel that a lowly son of dusk
Could move to tears the hardened soul of greed,
And crown his massive brow with laurel wreath.
His heart rejoiced when war destroyed the chains
That kept to earth his brothers of the dusk,
And when the sun of Freedom shone awhile
He marched abreast with Toil to save his race.
Ah! hear the bells a-ringing through the world,
"The slave is free! Grim bondage dies to-night!"
O blessed war, that saved humanity,
That gave the men of dusk the freemen's right,
How many sons of Ethiop were thine!
How many fell with Shaw ere peace returned!
Their graves unknown, who strews for them sweet flowers?
Who keeps their memory with incense fresh?
How many when young Cuba, lashed by Spain,
A greater country saved, were lost at war!
No truer soldiers live than men of dusk,
No better lovers of the starry flag.
No hope is theirs but welfare of the world,
No honours for the fighters of the dusk,
Are these rewards, O great America?
Obscurity, oppression, bitter scorn,
The right to serve, but never right to share.
Give us our liberty or give us death!

V.

And now that Freedom's orb so brightly burns
From crimson clay in old Virginia soil
Sweet Nature moulds another Washington;

Upon his brow she sets a flaming star,
Upon his lips the fire that never dies,
And smiles when men before his gospel bow,—
"The hand of toil alone will rule the world."
O Washington, may day upon us break!
May great America at last be free,
And true democracy where work is law
A common gift to all humanity.
Tuskegee's glory through the ages lives,
The light that makes Columbia a queen
Among the toiling nations of the earth,
Tuskegee stands a stone in Jacob's dream,
A ladder leading to the Gates of Pearl,—
And Washington alone hath laid the stone.

VI.

There sits aloft among the jaspar gates
Far famed the brooding spirit of his race,
A gentle soul by grim injustice wracked,
He looks in vain for hope, though he is hope.
O Ethiopia, in him thy King,
Thy weaver of the vision glorious,
Thy lover begging for thy liberty.
When Nature moulded him she chose a clay
So fine it could not bear a cruel storm;
But shaped his ponderous brow for laurel wreath.
In ages yet unborn the child of dusk
In reverence shall bow to Burghardt's name,
And all the world shall love a patriot.

VII.

O sons of Libya, thy name will live
The bearers of the Cross on Calvary;
Around thee wrapt the mantle of the dusk,
In thee the world will find another dawn,
Around thee shall the hour of twilight glow,
When day upon thee breaks a golden throne
Awaits thee in the land of rising sun,

Thy faith, thy deeds, thy love for fellow men
Shall be thy sceptre and thy coronet,
Before thee shall the vaunting nations bow
In reverence to crowned humility.

And thus I sing the song of Ethiop
Though I am dwelling in a stranger's land,
A lonely minstrel, born to serve and love
Throughout the world his fellows of the dusk.

Douglass.

He came when tyranny was ripe, a torch
That lit the darkened avenue of hope,
He came from cabin, ragged, poor, and starved,
And walked among the honoured of the earth.
His cry the cry of Moses to the King,
"Oh, let my people go, thou freeborn host,
For God hath heard their cry; they must be free."
He walked not shrouded, but with manhood stride,
The morning of a people long oppressed,
He stood within the palace of the King
And cried, "Give them their rights; they must be free.
These lowly folks,—my brothers, ay, thine, too,
Let not a democratic people cringe
To selfish idols, childish prejudice,
Let not the future ages note this land
That broke the chains Hanover's puppet forged
Enslaves and keeps enslaved a helpless race,
Whose hand has never struck the stars and stripes."
Ah! there was Phillips; there was Sumner, too,
With Lowell, Garrison, and Whittier,
And Brown, whose noble life Virginia took,
And Stowe, whose pen awoke the slumbering North;
But none of Afric line as bold as he,
As fiery and inveterate of speech,
As monumental of the intellect
A man of dusk may have, tho' born in chains—
A worthy peer for such a company.
When chaos ruled, and freedmen knew not where
The star of fortune would abide with them
This Douglass, dauntless as the wind of March,
As shepherd guides his sheep o'er stony crags
He guided long his race, all bruised and torn,
And faltering because the night was dark;
Until he heard the still small voice of Death

And drifted down the endless stream of Time.
O Douglass, thou hast left a heritage
To those whose brows are pierced by thorned crowns
And from thy couch in green Elysium
Where thou and Sumner and the laurelled Grant
And Ingersoll and Lincoln watch the tide,
Thy voice comes down to us, thy bleeding sheep.
And these thy words, O Prophet of the Dusk!
"Go on, my Race, the sun will rise again,
The Night will fade as darkness ever fades.
No race can always bend beneath the yoke,
For 'tis a truth the wrath of those oppressed
Will break the reins, and drink of liberty.
Be valiant, true, and know not cowardice
And live so that both friend and foe may say,
"Oh they were great in adversity
But greater in the hour of jubilee!"

Thus speaks our Douglass from his grave, and we
Should heed his mighty voice, lest we should fail.

Declaration.

I love the world and all therein:
The panting, darkened souls who seek
A brighter light, a sweeter hope,
From those who drink the bubbling wine
And eat the flesh of tender fowl;
I love the pampered son of wealth,
And pour on him my pity's oil,
This world our God hath made for all,—
The East, the West, the black, the white,
The rich, the poor, the wise, the dumb,—
And even beasts may share the fruit;
No prison wall, but sunlight's glow,
No rods of steel, but arms of love,
For all that creep and walk and strive
And wear upon their countenance
Creation's mark, the kiss of God.

Comin' Home.

1.

Oh, Ah hyeahs de ol' tahm bells a-ringin',
    Comin' home! Comin' home!
Sweetuh dan de angel hahp de singin',
    Comin' home! Comin' home!
Bu'dens dat Ah's toted fifty yeahs
Ah has laid away wid foolish teahs,
To de skies Ah raise mah weary eyes
An' to Dinah honey long Ah cries
    Comin' home! Comin' home!

2.

Oh, Ah hyeahs de ol' tahm folk a-callin',
    Comin' home! Comin' home!
Cross de Jawdon shadders gently fallin',
    Comin' home! Comin' home!
Down de stream dey float de ol' flat boat,
Songs ob sorrer comin' f'om daih th'oat,
Dey is gwine to tote mah soul away
Whaih de moonlight tu'ns de night to day,
    Comin' home! Comin' home!

The Banjo Player

There is music in me, the music of a peasant people.

I wander through the levee, picking my banjo and singing my songs of the cabin and the field. At the Last Chance Saloon I am as welcome as the violets in March; there is always food and drink for me there, and the dimes of those who love honest music. Behind the railroad tracks the little children clap their hands and love me as they love Kris Kringle.

But I fear that I am a failure. Last night a woman called me a troubadour. What is a troubadour?

The Scarlet Woman

Once I was good like the Virgin Mary and the Minister's wife.

My father worked for Mr. Pullman and white people's tips; but he died two days after his insurance expired.

I had nothing, so I had to go to work.

All the stock I had was a white girl's education and a face that enchanted the men of both races.

Starvation danced with me.

So when Big Lizzie, who kept a house for white men, came to me with tales of fortune that I could reap from the sale of my virtue I bowed my head to Vice.

Now I can drink more gin than any man for miles around.

Gin is better than all the water in Lethe.

The Minister

I mastered pastoral theology, the Greek of the Apostles, and all the difficult subjects in a minister's curriculum.

I was as learned as any in this country when the Bishop ordained me.

And I went to preside over Mount Moriah, largest flock in the Conference.

I preached the Word as I felt it, I visited the sick and dying and comforted the afflicted in spirit.

I loved my work because I loved my God.

But I lost my charge to Sam Jenkins, who has not been to school four years in his life.

I lost my charge because I could not make my congregation shout.

And my dollar money was small, very small.

Sam Jenkins can tear a Bible to tatters and his congregation destroys the pews with their shouting and stamping.

Sam Jenkins leads in the gift of raising dollar money.

Such is religion.

Rulers: Philadelphia

It is said that many a king in troubled Europe would sell his
  crown for a day of happiness.
I have seen a monarch who held tightly the jewel of happiness.
On Lombard Street in Philadelphia, as evening dropped to
  earth, I gazed upon a laborer duskier than a sky devoid of
  moon. He was seated on a throne of flour bags, waving
  his hand imperiously as two small boys played on their
  guitars the ragtime tunes of the day.
God's blessing on the monarch who rules on Lombard Street
  in Philadelphia.

Aunt Hannah Jackson

Despite her sixty years Aunt Hannah Jackson rubs on other people's clothes.

Time has played havoc with her eyes and turned to gray her parched hair.

But her tongue is nimble as she talks to herself.

All day she talks to herself about her neighbors and her friends and the man she loved.

Yes, Aunt Hannah Jackson loved even as you and I and Wun Hop Sing.

"He was a good man," she says, "but a fool."

"So am I a fool and Mrs. Lee a fool and this Mrs. Goldstein that I work for a fool."

"All of us are fools."

For rubbing on other people's clothes Aunt Hannah Jackson gets a dollar and fifty cents a day and a worn out dress on Christmas.

For talking to herself Aunt Hannah Jackson gets a smile as we call her a good natured fool.

Aunt Jane Allen

State Street is lonely to-day. Aunt Jane Allen has driven her chariot to Heaven.

I remember how she hobbled along, a little woman, parched of skin, brown as the leather of a satchel and with eyes that had scanned eighty years of life.

Have those who bore her dust to the last resting place buried with her the basket of aprons she went up and down State Street trying to sell?

Have those who bore her dust to the last resting place buried with her the gentle word Son that she gave to each of the seed of Ethiopia?

Tired

I am tired of work; I am tired of building up somebody else's civilization.

Let us take a rest, M'Lissy Jane.

I will go down to the Last Chance Saloon, drink a gallon or two of gin, shoot a game or two of dice and sleep the rest of the night on one of Mike's barrels.

You will let the old shanty go to rot, the white people's clothes turn to dust, and the Calvary Baptist Church sink to the bottomless pit.

You will spend your days forgetting you married me and your nights hunting the warm gin Mike serves the ladies in the rear of the Last Chance Saloon.

Throw the children into the river; civilization has given us too many. It is better to die than it is to grow up and find out that you are colored.

Pluck the stars out of the heavens. The stars mark our destiny. The stars marked my destiny.

I am tired of civilization.

GEORGIA DOUGLAS JOHNSON

Selections from
Bronze: A Book of Verse (1922)

The work of the playwright, music teacher, and poet Georgia Douglas Johnson (1880–1966) represents a core element of our commitment to *Minor Notes*. That is, not only the recuperation of poets who are relatively unknown across history, but those who were exceedingly well known in their time and since seem to have fallen out of the popular consciousness.

Johnson is an example of the latter. She was, in no uncertain terms, the most widely read black woman poet in the United States during the first three decades of the twentieth century. Her second book of poems, *Bronze: A Book of Verse*, was introduced with a foreword by W. E. B. Du Bois. She wrote twenty-eight plays, and about that many songs, in addition to her remarkable output in the realm of poetry, fiction, and nonfiction (she wrote both a book of stories and a biography of her late husband).

Beyond her work on the page, Johnson was also a culture worker who always created spaces wherein other black writers could flourish. Perhaps the most striking example of this is her opening her home in Washington, DC—which she playfully dubbed "the Half-way House," but which was more commonly referred to as the "S Street Salon"—to artists such as Langston Hughes, Zora Neale Hurston, and Jean Toomer. In 1965, she was presented with an honorary doctorate in literature from Atlanta University. She died the next year. Her legacy—in this project and elsewhere—lives on.

Black Woman

Don't knock at my door, little child,
    I cannot let you in,
You know not what a world this is
    Of cruelty and sin.
Wait in the still eternity
    Until I come to you,
The world is cruel, cruel, child,
    I cannot let you in!

Don't knock at my heart, little one,
    I cannot bear the pain
Of turning deaf-ear to your call
    Time and time again!
You do not know the monster men
    Inhabiting the earth,
Be still, be still, my precious child,
    I must not give you birth!

Sonnet to Those Who See but Darkly

Their gaze uplifting from shoals of despair
Like phantoms groping enswathed from the light
Up from miasmic depths, children of night,
Surge to the piping of Hope's dulcet lay,
Souled like the lily, whose splendors declare
God's mazèd paradox—purged of all blight,
Out from the quagmire, unsullied and fair.

Life holds her arms o'er the festering way,
Smiles, as their faith-sandalled rushes prevail,
Slowly the sun rides the marge of the day,
Wine to the lips sorely anguished and pale;
On, ever on, do the serried ranks sway
Charging the ultimate, rending the veil.

Perspective

Some day
I shall be glad that it was mine to be
A dark fore-runner of a race burgeoning;
I then shall know
The secret of life's Calvary,
And bless the thorns
That wound me!

Cosmopolite

Not wholly this or that,
But wrought
Of alien bloods am I,
A product of the interplay
Of traveled hearts.
Estranged, yet not estranged, I stand
All comprehending;
From my estate
I view earth's frail dilemma;
Scion of fused strength am I,
All understanding,
Nor this nor that
Contains me.

Laocoön

This spirit-choking atmosphere
  With deadly serpent-coil
Entwines my soaring-upwardness
  And chains me to the soil,
Where'er I seek with eager stride
  To gain yon gleaming height,
These noisesome fetters coil aloft
  And snare my buoyant flight.

O, why these aspirations bold,
  These rigours of desire,
That surge within so ceaselessly
  Like living tongues of fire?
And why these glowing forms of hope
  That scintillate and shine,
If naught of all that burnished dream
  Can evermore be mine?

It cannot be, fate does not mock,
  And man's untoward decree
Shall not forever thus confine
  My life's entirety,
My every fibre fierce rebels
  Against this servile role,
And all my being broods to break
  This death-grip from my soul!

We Face the Future

The hour is big with sooth and sign, with errant men at war,
While blood of alien, friend, and foe imbues the land afar,
And we, with sable faces pent, move with the vanguard line,
Shod with a faith that Springtime keeps, and all the stars opine.

To Samuel Coleridge Taylor, upon Hearing His "Sometimes I Feel Like a Motherless Child"

Strange to a sensing motherhood,
Loved as a toy—not understood,
Child of a dusky father, bold;
Frail little captive, exiled, cold.

Oft when the brooding planets sleep,
You through their drowsy empires creep,
Flinging your arms through their empty space,
Seeking the breast of an unknown face.

The Measure

Fierce is the conflict—the battle of eyes,
Sure and unerring, the wordless replies,
Challenges flash from their ambushing caves—
Men, by their glances, are masters or slaves.

Shall I Say, "My Son, You're Branded"?

Shall I say, "My son, you're branded in this country's pageantry,
By strange subtleties you're tethered, and no forum sets you
    free?"
Shall I mark the young lights fading through your soul-
    enchannelled eye,
As the dusky pall of shadows screen the highway of your sky?

Or shall I, with love prophetic, bid you dauntlessly arise,
Spurn the handicap that clogs you, taking what the world denies,
Bid you storm the sullen fortress wrought by prejudice and wrong
With a faith that shall not falter, in your heart and on your
    tongue!

Common Dust

And who shall separate the dust
Which later we shall be:
Whose keen discerning eye will scan
And solve the mystery?

The high, the low, the rich, the poor,
The black, the white, the red,
And all the chromatique between,
Of whom shall it be said:

Here lies the dust of Africa;
Here are the sons of Rome;
Here lies one unlabelled,
The world at large his home!

Can one then separate the dust,
Will mankind lie apart,
When life has settled back again
The same as from the start?

Old Black Men

They have dreamed as young men dream
Of glory, love and power;
They have hoped as youth will hope
Of life's sun-minted hour.

They have seen as others saw
Their bubbles burst in air,
And they have learned to live it down
As though they did not care.

The Heart of a Woman

The heart of a woman goes forth with the dawn,
As a lone bird, soft winging, so restlessly on,
Afar o'er life's turrets and vales does it roam
In the wake of those echoes the heart calls home.

The heart of a woman falls back with the night,
And enters some alien cage in its plight,
And tries to forget it has dreamed of the stars
While it breaks, breaks, breaks on the sheltering bars.

HENRIETTA CORDELIA RAY

Selections from *Sonnets* (1893)

Like many of the black poets active in the years after Emancipation, Henrietta Cordelia Ray (1852–1916) was also a teacher. She was born in New York City and taught in the New York City school system for thirty years, notably in the girl's section of Colored Grammar School No. 1 (located at 135 Mulberry Street) and in the 1890s at No. 80 (located at 252 West Forty-Second Street), where the prominent educator and mathematician Charles L. Reason (himself an occasional minor poet) served as principal.

Ray was born into a prominent abolitionist family. Her father, Charles Bennett Ray, was born free in Falmouth, Massachusetts, in 1807 and, in 1832, was the first black student to enroll at Wesleyan University, although he was unable to attend after white students protested his admission. He moved to New York, where he rose to prominence in the anti-slavery movement, cofounding the New York City Vigilance Committee, joining the American Anti-Slavery Society, becoming a key figure in the Underground Railroad's operations in the city, and taking up editorship of *The Colored American*, one of the earliest African American newspapers. His first wife, Henrietta Green Regulus (after whom Henrietta Cordelia was named), was likewise an abolitionist activist, notable for her work with the African Dorcas Association, a black women's mutual aid society. Cordelia's sister, Charlotte E. Ray, was the first black woman to graduate from Howard University Law

School and, in 1872, the first black woman admitted to the District of Columbia bar.

Cordelia Ray (as she preferred to be known) came to prominence when she presented her eighty-line ode "Lincoln" on April 14, 1876, in Washington, DC, at the commemorative events celebrating the Emancipation Proclamation and the unveiling of Thomas Ball's bronze Emancipation Memorial statue in Lincoln Park. She continued to write poetry throughout the 1880s and 1890s, publishing *Sonnets* in 1893 and *Poems* in 1910.

Toussaint L'Ouverture

To those fair isles where crimson sunsets burn,
We send a backward glance to gaze on thee,
Brave Toussaint! thou wast surely born to be
A hero; thy proud spirit could but spurn
Each outrage on thy race. Couldst thou unlearn
The lessons taught by instinct? Nay! and we
Who share the zeal that would make all men free,
Must e'en with pride unto thy life-work turn.
Soul-dignity was thine and purest aim;
And ah! how sad that thou wast left to mourn
In chains 'neath alien skies. On him, shame! shame!
That mighty conqueror who dared to claim
The right to bind thee. Him we heap with scorn,
And noble patriot! guard with love thy name.

Aspiration.

We climb the slopes of life with throbbing heart,
   And eager pulse, like children toward a star.
   Sweet siren music cometh from afar,
To lure us on meanwhile. Responsive start
The nightingales to richer song than Art
   Can ever teach. No passing shadows mar
   Awhile the dewy skies; no inner jar
Of conflict bids us with our quest to part.
We see adown the distance, rainbow-arched,
   What melting aisles of liquid light and bloom!
We hasten, tremulous, with lips all parched,
   And eyes wide-stretched, nor dream of coming gloom.
Enough that something held almost divine
Within us ever stirs. Can we repine?

Self-Mastery.

To catch the spirit in its wayward flight
   Through mazes manifold, what task supreme!
   For when to floods has grown the quiet stream,
Much human skill must aid its rage to fight;
And when wild winds invade the solemn night,
   Seems not man's vaunted power but a dream?
   And still more futile, ay, we e'en must deem
This quest to tame the soul, and guide aright
Its restless wanderings,—to lure it back
   To shoals of calm. Full many a moan and sigh
      Attend the strife: till, effort merged in prayer,
Oft uttered, clung to—when of strength the lack
   Seems direst—brings the answer to our cry:
      A gift from Him who lifts our ev'ry care.

Limitations

The subtlest strain a great musician weaves,
Cannot attain in rhythmic harmony
To music in his soul. May it not be
Celestial lyres send hints to him? He grieves
That half the sweetness of the song, he leaves
Unheard in the transition. Thus do we
Yearn to translate the wondrous majesty
Of some rare mood, when the rapt soul receives
A vision exquisite. Yet who can match
The sunset's iridescent hues? Who sing
The skylark's ecstasy so seraph-fine?
We struggle vainly, still we fain would catch
Such rifts amid life's shadows, for they bring
Glimpses ineffable of things divine.

The Poet's Ministrants.

The smiling Dawn, with diadem of dew,
   Brings sunrise odors to perfume his shrine;
   Blithe Zephyr fans him, and soft moonbeams twine
An aureole to crown him, of a hue
Surpassing fair. The stately stars renew
   Majestic measures, that he may incline
   His soul unto their sweetness; whispers fine
From spirit-nymphs allure him; not a few
The gifts chaste Fancy and her sisters bring.
   Rare is the lyre the Muses for him wrought,
A different meaning thrills in ev'ry string,
   With ev'ry changing mood of life so fraught.
Invoked by him, when such the strains that flow,
How can the poet e'er his song forego!

Milton.

O poet gifted with the sight divine!
   To thee 'twas given Eden's groves to pace
   With that first pair, in whom the human race
Their kinship claim: and angels did incline—
Great Michael, holy Gabriel—to twine
   Their heavenly logic, through which thou couldst trace
   The rich outpourings of celestial grace
Mingled with argument, around the shrine
Where thou didst linger, vision-rapt, intent
   To catch the sacred mystery of Heaven.
      Nor was thy longing vain: a soul resolved
To ponder truth supreme to thee was lent;
   For thy not *sightless* eyes the veil was riv'n,
      Redemption's problem unto thee well solved.

In Memoriam
Paul Laurence Dunbar

The Muse of Poetry came down one day,
And brought with willing hands a rare, sweet gift;
She lingered near the cradle of a child,
Who first unto the sun his eyes did lift.
She touched his lips with true Olympian fire,
And at her bidding Fancies hastened there,
To flutter lovingly around the one
So favored by the Muse's gentle care.

Who was this child? The offspring of a race
That erst had toiled 'neath slavery's galling chains.
And soon he woke to utterance and sang
In sweetly cadenced and in stirring strains,
Of simple joys, and yearnings, and regrets;
Anon to loftier themes he turned his pen;
For so in tender, sympathetic mood
He caught the follies and the griefs of men.

His tones were various: we list, and lo!
"Malindy Sings," and as the echoes die,
The keynote changes and another strain
Of solemn majesty goes floating by;
And sometimes in the beauty and the grace
Of an impassioned, melancholy lay,
We seem to hear the surge, and swell, and moan
Of soft orchestral music far away.

Paul Dunbar dead! His genius cannot die!
It lives in songs that thrill, and glow, and soar;
Their pathos and their joy will fill our hearts,
And charm and satisfy e'en as of yore.

So when we would lament our poet gone,
With sorrow that his lyre is resting now,
Let us remember, with the fondest pride,
That Fame's immortal wreath has crowned his brow.

Ode on the Twentieth Century
(A Dream-Prophecy.)

What seer is this,
Who gazing calm athwart the deep
Where pent-up storms and thunders sleep,
    Nothing can miss?
O'er sweeping with his falcon glance vast tracks,
Chaotic, dim, mysterious.
    What lacks
His prescience brooding o'er a cycle new?
What vaster view
Saw ever seer of eld wrapped in a trance?
What pageant more majestic to enhance
His spirit's yearning mood?
    To distant caves
    The mighty ocean laves,
To airy grottoes, where the lightning wakes,
His searching glance is sent.
Serene, absorbed, attent,
    He meditates;
Forecasting what may be in days unborn—
Days that with sunrise freshness all impearled,
    With wings unfurled,
Pause to alight upon a waiting world.

"What may they bring us, Seer?
    Unto thy vision clear
    Is all revealed?
What of those mystic spheres
    Th' unfathomable years
So close have sealed?
What cult is taught in Venus?
    Shall we know
Whether there come and go

Fair mortals on that soil unknown,
To manly stature grown?
Are hearth-fires kindled on that planet-isle,
And o'er the sacred pile
Does incense rise to some Divinity?
Look closer, Seer, and see!"

O the wonder of the vision!
O the marvel of the sight!
What shores and streams Elysian!
What scenes with splendor dight!
The seer is rapt: enkindled
His brooding glance has grown;
Then solemn made he answer,
With myst'ry in his tone.

"I grope: the scales are yet
Upon my asking eyes;
Forebodings of surprise
My spirit seize; then let
Naught rude disturb my consecrated mood.

.   .   .   .   .

"'Tis come! 'tis come! the vision grows apace!
The scales have fall'n, and behold! I trace
    Wonders sublime;
    The scroll of Time
With deeper mysteries will be o'er-writ.

"The world is spanned by bridges
Builded of rainbow rays;
O'er foam and wat'ry ridges,
They glitter, glitter to the moon.
They'll lead the foot full soon
To dwellings past the Pleiads,
To Cassiope's bright seat.
A thought! and lo, we gaze
Amid a planet's haze.
Could motion be more fleet?

"And harken! Down the chiming spheres
To list'ning ears,
An anthem comes from Jupiter's vast plain—
A matchless strain.

   "A message from a star!
   Harness the wingèd car
With other steeds than any seen before.
Why heed our lagging pow'rs?
   Star-wisdom will be ours;
E'en in a flash of thought
   Intelligence be brought,
   Undreamed of lore.

"I see a hall of weird magnificence,
All studded o'er with scintillating gems
Of rarest lustre; 'tis a temple whence
Flows wisdom like a river; nothing stems
The rushing of its richly freighted waves.
Lo! 'tis on Saturn's isles where stately stands
That gleaming hall, and countless student bands
Are flocking thither in air-chariots brought
To learn the subtlest thought
   Of star and planet lore,
   All unrevealed before.

"Wisdom from worlds erstwhile beyond our ken.
Stupendous! marvelous! what deeds of men
Evoke this guerdon? Lo! the Deity
Makes man to praise
His boundless majesty.
These works beyond compare
   His signet bear.

"And all the alchemy of Earth's vast depths,
Magic in coruscating jewels hid,
Secrets but vaguely hinted by the winds,
Marvels beneath the Ocean's wavy lid,

Have yielded to man's craving; myst'ries sealed
Since sun and moon and stars from Chaos wheeled,
    Are now revealed.

"I cease to gaze. I cannot struggle more
With mighty sights and sounds that wingèd come
From space illimitable, and my eyes
Grow misty 'neath th' effulgence. I am dumb.
I cannot fathom what so near me lies—
Wonders unseen, unheard, unknown before."
The curtain falls again, the quest is o'er.

DAVID WADSWORTH CANNON JR.

Selections from *Black Labor Chant* (1939)

In his brief life, David Wadsworth Cannon Jr. (1910–1938) was known as a poet, a musician, a gifted educator, and a burgeoning scholar. He was born in New Brunswick, New Jersey, and died prematurely in 1938 from a sudden illness as he was completing a study on the expectations and experiences of black students in HBCUs as partial fulfillment toward a degree of a PhD at Teachers College, Columbia University, in New York City. He was raised in New Brunswick by his mother, a social worker, and his father, a Baptist minister and graduate of Lincoln University and Princeton Theological Seminary. Cannon received his BA from Hillsdale College in Michigan in 1931 and an MA in psychology from the University of Michigan in 1932. During his time in Michigan, he briefly pastored in a rural white church.

With his degree in hand, he was appointed as an assistant professor in psychology and education on the faculty of Virginia State College in Petersburg. He lectured, taught, and served community projects like the state's adult education program, church school classes, and the direction of the college's student verse-speaking choir, which completed two concert tours in 1937 and 1938, including stops in New York City. Eager to pursue his studies and obtain an advanced degree, Cannon applied for and was awarded a Julius Rosenwald Fund fellowship in 1937 to pursue a doctorate in educational psychology at Columbia University.

Cannon was writing poetry during his time at Virginia State College and most likely earlier as well. Upon his death, his mother, Gertrude Cannon, gathered his writings, and with the support of the National Council on Religion in Higher Education, his friends and family arranged to posthumously publish his only poetry collection, *Black Labor Chant*, in 1939. This remarkable book is illustrated by the poet's friend John Borican and includes brief lyrics, work songs composed for the student verse-choir at Virginia State that show the influence of Sterling Brown's *Southern Road* (1932), spiritual meditations inspired in some cases by a summer trip to tour the landscapes of the US Southwest, and "protest" poems influenced by the Popular Front aesthetic that animated black poets during the years of the Great Depression. Unfortunately, Cannon never got the chance to fully see his talent and promise develop, and his minor place in the landscape of black poetry has much to do with the abrupt end of his life and the fact that his poetry wasn't placed with a literary publisher. *Black Labor Chant* is a stained-glass window showing the nascent yearnings of a black poet and educator in the 1930s grappling with the possibilities of modernist vernacular poetics, religious temperament, uplift zeal, and a flinty commitment to social protest.

I.

LABOR CHANTS

Black Labor Chant

Largo: Cry pine!
        I pierce you through for turpentine,
        To heal the white man's wounds.

Staccato: Squeak barrel!
        Swing cargo!
        I push you,
          throw you,
          shove you,
        Into white men's deep black boats!

Forte: Break rock!
        Crack stone!
        I mash you into road powder, house paste,—
        For rich men's homes!

        Grow cotton!
        Burst cotton!
        I pick you!
        Send you to great black mill!
        To make white sheets,
        For Ku Klux Klan
        To hang me with!

        Melt iron!
        Blaze steel!

I pour you into bridge-ribs,
                    car tracks,
                    long straight guns,
That hunt me, shoot me,—make me good!

Presto-   Burn light!
vivace: Cut drill!
             To make coal dust for white men's trains!
             I taste it, in his "jim crow" car.

(leader)   Cut!
(gang)   I bleed pine to heal the white men's wounds!

(leader)   Shove!
(gang)   I throw freight into white men's boats!

(leader)   Swing!
(gang)   I mash rock into white men's roads!

(leader)   Heave!
(gang)   I mould guns which shoot me down!

(leader)   Bend!
(gang)   I make sheets which snap my neck!

             So!
             Cry pine!
             Swing barrel!
             Break rock!
             Melt iron!
             Cut drill!
             Burn light!
             Black—
             Men—
             Work!

"Freedom in Mah Soul"

I.

Fo'ty acres jes' fo' me!
And freedom in mah soul!
Great pines lickin' up de sky,
Hickories too and oaks so high,
And freedom in mah soul!

I can see it jes' as plain
As if it all was done now.
Fo'ty acres, mule an' plow—
Cabin big enuf fo' foah,
Garden 'fo' mah own front do',
And freedom in mah soul!

Den we gotta dig a well
Deep, so she'll be plenty cool,
Next we're goin' to raise a church,
And den, we'll build a school.
Lawd, if dis ain't jes' too grand,
Led us straight to de promised land,
Freedom in mah soul.

II.

Come on men!
Let's cut 'em down.
Come on men!
Let's clear dis ground!

Swing! . . .
Swing! . . .
Freedom in yo' soul?
Yas! . . .
Swing! . . .

Swing! . . .
Freedom in our souls!

Gotta cut deeper
Won't be long.
Gotta cut deeper
Hit it strong!
Swing! . . .
Swing! . . .
Freedom's in mah soul!

III.

Now, let's clear dese stumps away,
'Cause we ain't got no time to play.
Freedom's in mah soul!

Giddy-up, Maude, now come on gal,
Pull dat stump away dere!
Easy dere, now pull right hard,
Pull dat stump away dere!
Guess dis whip will set you right,
Dis patch must be cleared 'fo' night.
Freedom in mah soul! . . .
Lawd! It sho' is burnin' hot.
Maude, now give de best you've got
'Cause we ain't got no time to play,
Gotta clear dese stumps away.
Freedom in mah soul!

Well, praise de Lawd!
She's jes' 'bout clear
And read fo' de cabin.
Is freedom in yo' soul?
Come on men, let's lift 'em up!
We'll raise a side 'fo' sundown.
Come on men,
Let's chunk 'em up!

So dat she sits smug on de ground!
We'll raise a side 'fo' sundown.

Heave! . . .
Heave! . . .
Heave! . . .
Freedom in yo' soul?
Heave! . . .
Heave! . . .
Heave! . . .
Freedom in mah soul!
Hammer her in! . . .
Cradle her so!

Hammer her in! . . .
Hit her some mo'! . . .
Freedom's in mah soul!

Long she'll stand!
Mah cabin, mine!
Yes dis is de promised land!
Trees! . . .
Woods! . . .
Hills! . . .
Lawd! . . .
Freedom's in mah soul!

"UNDER THE HAWTHORN TREE"

Old Faithful

Old
Faithful
really is
the devil's clock,
which ticks on slowly
till just one hour is spent.
Then bootlegger or bishop,
as the case may be, winds it up.
Hot water, gas, sulphur fumes spurt out!
to give one just a glimpse of hell.
It quiets down and ticks right on
until another hour.
Then strikes again—
to warn all
sinful
men.

Western Town

Dry Gap—a dingy general store.
A sign said, "Population Seven."
I found a universe for two:
One sun, one moon, and called it heaven.

Cheyenne Fiddler

Bar maids, pipe smoke, and sleazy air—
Two cowboys drunk. A tawdry pair
of wenches pawed at them for pay
well earned. One fellow tried to say,
"Get down!" The second cursed till all
the others laughed. A sun-seared tall
ole man started fiddlin' while the fun
was high. He and the hall were one.

A battered hat crouched on his head.
Wild strands of hair stood out, and led
the way to eyes which burned like stars
on fire beneath a brow of scars—
each one the memory of a fight
to death. His face, parched skin drawn tight
across a frame of bones. The sun
was low. Fiddle and he were one.

The squeaky box gave birth to bark
of coyote, wail of wolf, the stark
quick rise of sage hen from the brush.
A short dry rattle; then the hush
of night; the tang of plains; the smell
of scorching hide at round-up. Well
had he lived his day. The tune was done.
The dream, the song, and he were one.

Western Plains

Aeons ago when stars were young,
before the first bird ever sung
a note, before the moon was cold,
mountains of ice and snow caught hold
of rocks and slowly cut their hearts away,
leaving their bodies buried deep in clay.
The dark brown clumps of dry sage brush
still marked the graves; and at the hush
of dawn the strident bellow of a steer
sounds reveille to life. And here
brown billows rise, wind tossed and free,
crest upon crest, as if a sea
gone mad, had lost its placid blue
and raging, turned to darker hue.
Two sage hens strut across a trail
which dreams of buffalo and pale
moons shining on a tribal war.
A rattler stirs! In Indian lore
a thing of charm to bring the rain.
And year on year, the hot red pain
of sun fire will sear land and sky—
Aeons from now, when old stars die.

Canyon Pain

For torpid lips and ghost thin gasping sighs,
The sweet cool elixir of pale lush green.
For dreamless, soulless hot and empty eyes,
Soft spongy blues, westwindwashed clear and clean—
Sore feet, hide bound, light blind, are free to tread
The mist cooled dustiness of red chilled pink.
A shattered heart seeks wholeness in a thread
Of net sea-foam, spun from the river's brink.

Then, curved wet lips did frame a lover's song
And liquid eyes reflect a far off dream.
Soft mellow hands fluted the whole day long,
While eager feet did leap o'er each moonbeam.
Now, they are still. The foam threads burst in twain.
I only feel the throb of canyon pain.

Mountains

The weight of mountains is upon me.
Tall stretching pines, pregnant with cone, yawn with
    the swaying bodies of their unborn kind.
Only the west wind understood.
Full well, he knew their backs would bend
    with cushioned cloud weight earthward.
That they would only know the
    same dark valleys that their forebears knew.

Yet, he was free to roam—
To sense the ecstasy of life . . .
And never feel the pallid hand of Death.

Peaks pinch soft clouds!
And they—young virgins of a wind swept day—did
    weep and knew not why.
Flowers caught their tears—
    Such wet pain is the meat of flowered laughter.

Snows hugged bold young summits.
Old spinsters!
Vainly snatching love from youth
    lest they should die ere they knew life—
A frozen sterile union,
Which countless dawns and fervid twilights
    have not kindled into birth.

Pine, heavy with cone!
Peaks, cloud burdened!
Summits, snow weary!
The weight of mountains is upon me.

III.

"SYMBIOSIS"

Boston Tea

"The Ladies of the D. A. R.
Meet here today at four, for tea."
Malinda Attucks washed the plates,
And baked small cakes for thirty-three.

She smiled; and looked at Crispus Attucks,
"Black Martyr,—Independence War,"
Who mused in marble silence on the square . . .
Then, she served tea to thirty-four.

Resignation

A spear of sun-bright lacquered red
Shot down a spiral country road:
Aunt Chloe's only laying hen was dead.
Her voice fused with the shrieking brakes,
"De good Lawd gives, but de white folks takes."

Tree Surgery

This was no sudden silence of the heart!
Three generations' eyes again gleamed red.
"Dis rope might bruise de bark, and scar de tree."
"We'll cut it, soon as he 'drops dead.'"

Representation

They were so proud of twenty spires!
The whole town understood
Why twenty devotees were there,
With sacrificial rope and hood.

Transfer of Training

Poor Mose! Why should he fear his master's ghost
When he comes home from work each night?
For it can read, and loyally obey the sign
Above the gate, which says, "For White."

Theology

Scene: Mission School—South
Characters: White teacher, Negro pupils

"The streets up there are paved with gold.
The sun shines day and night."
"Miss Lee, could I git in and stay?"
"What?"
"Ain't God un angels white?"

Predestination

"Lullubelle!"
"Yaas'm."
"Git right down fum dat rock pile.
Come right heah!"
"Did you hit Major Johnson's chile?
Tell de truth!"
"Yaas'm. He called me nigger,
And climbed a tree."
"Go right on.
Tell me mo'!"
"A rock was lookin' straight at me!"
"Go long, chile!"
"Yaas'm."

Auntie's Notion

Chile—
When I dies,
don't put no cold white statue ovah me!
Cause all my life
I'se longed to git away from white folks—
And be free to do de things
mah soul has hankered fo'.

To stretch out straight
beneath a weepin' willow tree
and doze . . .
Chile when I dies,
don't put no cold white statue ovah me.

Native Intelligence

(Scene: On a Bus)

The blind man entered from the "darkened" rear.
A Negro offered him a seat. He stood,—
Until the driver led him to a place
In front, to sit where white men should!

Bank Porter

8 A.M.
"Last night, I dreamed I was in hell.
(I eat too much and don't sleep well.)
Now Rastus, what's that mean for me?"
"De good Lawd shows us what's to be!"

10 A.M.
Two shots, a third, a woman's scream . . .
"I'se glad dat I don't nevah dream!"

Proof

I usta work fo' real blue bloods,
I served 'em cocktails all night long.
When dey stahted pullin' off dere clothes, I left.
Next day de missus axed me what was wrong.

Pok Chops

"Pok chops, for supper?"
"Umph huh, son!
I'll make a nice thick gravy,
Soon as dey gits right done."
"Say ma, ole Major died!
And didn't name his heir."
"What? No chile!
Well, I declare—
And me a cookin' pok chops
Fo' a millionaire."

Liberty Bond

First Person Plural
(*Scene:* Bank—South)

"What can I do fo' you all this mornin', Lucy?"
"De mistress say de sheriff's gonta sell her place.
I wants to sell mah fifty dollar war bond,
So as to help to keep us from disgrace."

Ad Infinitum

Night riders burned their cornfield down.
Content,—they could not rise from such a loss . . .
Yet, where a scarecrow once had stood
They knelt beneath the shadow of a cross!

Eclipse

Black Boy!
White seers claim your course is run.
Move on!
And when this epoch's done
Stand in the pathway of the sun!

Orthodoxy

Scene: Court Room—South
Characters: White divorcée's lawyer, his client,
and her Negro maid

"Matilda Williams will you take the chair?
You swear to tell the truth and just the truth?"

"Just what I knows, dats all dat I can swear."

"Now, did he have the key to the front door?"

"I don't know, suh. It's mighty hard for me to see
When I'm pickin' footprints off de flo'."

"That night at ten, then, did you hear a knock?"

"No suh, I says mah prayers and gits in bed,
Lord knows, I'm fast asleep by nine o'clock."

"When he came did the door bell ever ring?"

"Ma room is over de white folks garage,
And, I can nevah hear a single thing."

"Matilda! Thanks to you, I know I'll win!"

"Umph! My Grandma taught me when I was a chile,
Not knowin' white folks business never was no sin!"

IV

MISCELLANEOUS POEMS

Pigment

Delores . . .

Your face
Robs apple blossoms of their hue,
Is clear
As crystal fairy-mirrored dew,
And fair
As half-ope'd water lily buds.

Dinah . . .

Your face
With tints of deep Etruscan bronze
Is soft
As frothy budding seaweed fronds
And dark
As mystic shadows are, at dusk.

Delores!

Your skin
Shall make the world kneel at your gate
And love you.

Dinah!

Your skin
Shall make the world pass by your gate
And hate you.

To Nita

You—
You are a forest, cool, lush, and green,
And I—
Only a little bird, lost in the arms of your smallest tree.
You—
You are a quaint old garden in springtime,
And I—
Only a bumblebee
Caught in a spider's web
Spun in your shyest flower.
You—
You are the sea at moonrise,
Placid—deep . . .
And I—
Only a silver fish fashioning a ripple—close,
Close near the heart of you.

World Weariness—"Weltschmerz"

I have grown weary of this carnal bark,
Of red tufted heart that drums a hollow bough.
The Lonely One was nailed upon a tree.
In every vein, I am as bruisèd now.
And yet, no storm can wash me out to sea.
My dying roots eke deeper than the earth.
Like Nicodemus, old and facing death,
They seek again the source of second birth.

When autumn came the frightened birds obeyed.
I was alone, and knew no song to sing.
And though this winter's fury whips me bare,
I know that I shall leaf another spring.

For I was living when this puny world
Leaped full-grown from the forehead of the sun.
I struggled through archean ooze and climbed
Upon the land, and I became as one
With all the silent crust-bound creeping things.

Then, weary of the earth, I wooed the sky . . .
And now again I seek the soft brown loam.
For though a hundred million years are spent,
I still remember nights when silver foam
From moon drenched lakes, was frothing at my feet.

I have grown weary of this carnal bark
I sense the pulse of aeons yet to be.
Push out strong rootlets, light-bound prisoned soul,
And wind yourself around infinity.

ANNE SPENCER

Selections from Uncollected Poems

Anne Spencer (1882–1975) loved to garden. It's important to begin with this particular facet of her daily creative practice, in part, because so many other aspects of her life flowed through it. Three separate monographs take up Spencer's garden as an organizing metaphor for their aims: a biography titled *Time's Unfading Garden: Anne Spencer's Life and Poetry* (1977), by J. Lee Greene; *Half My World: The Garden of Anne Spencer: A History and Guide* (2003), by Rebecca T. Frischkorn and Reuben M. Rainey; and *Lessons Learned from a Poet's Garden* (2011), by Jane Baber White.

The White text is a case study of the labor undertaken by members of the Hillside Garden Club over the course of twenty-eight years to restore, and sustain, her garden (which, alongside her home, is a Virginia landmark in the National Register of Historical Places). Spencer's home, in Lynchburg, Virginia, was a consistent place of gathering for the black intellectuals of her day; Marian Anderson, George Washington Carver, W. E. B. Du Bois, and others could be counted among her guests. Anne's garden was located behind the house, adjacent to a cottage and writing studio that her husband, Edward Alexander Spencer, built for her. They called it *Edankraal*: a combination of the couple's names and *kraal*, the Afrikaans word for "enclosure."

Spencer's commitment to the stewardship of the planet was not limited to her creative practice in the garden, however. In addition to her work therein, she was also a poet, teacher, activist, and librarian of Dunbar High School. Both her public and her literary work bear the trace of this capacious vision. Alongside her husband, Edward, her friend Mary Rice Hayes Allen, and several other colleagues including James Weldon Johnson, Spencer helped revive the Lynchburg chapter of the NAACP. Over the course of a fifty-three-year literary career, she would see her poems published in *The Crisis, The New Negro, Caroling Dusk, The Book of American Negro Poetry,* and *The Norton Anthology of Modern Poetry.* Her poems—which dance elegantly between topics ranging from the daily lives of flowers and bees to the global struggle against anti-black racism, refracted through the lens of ecological metaphor—come to us as a reminder in the present day that environmental concerns have always been at the core of the black expressive tradition. And that black poetry is, in one sense, a way for us to imagine the social worlds of forms of life that might otherwise fall beyond the bounds of our attention and, thus, our care.

At the Carnival

Gay little Girl-of-the-Diving-Tank,
I desire a name for you,
Nice, as a right glove fits;
For you—who amid the malodorous
Mechanics of this unlovely thing,
Are darling of spirit and form.
I know you—a glance, and what you are
Sits-by-the-fire in my heart.
My Limousine-Lady knows you, or
Why does the slant-envy of her eye mark
Your straight air and radiant inclusive smile?
Guilt pins a fig-leaf; Innocence is its own adorning.
The bull-necked man knows you—this first time
His itching flesh sees form divine and vibrant health
And thinks not of his avocation.
I came incuriously—
Set on no diversion save that my mind
Might safely nurse its brood of misdeeds
In the presence of a blind crowd.
The color of life was gray.
Everywhere the setting seemed right
For my mood.
Here the sausage and garlic booth
Sent unholy incense skyward;
There a quivering female-thing
Gestured assignations, and lied
To call it dancing;
There, too, were games of chance
With chances for none;
But oh! Girl-of-the-Tank, at last!
Gleaming Girl, how intimately pure and free
The gaze you send the crowd,
As though you know the dearth of beauty
In its sordid life.

We need you—my Limousine-Lady,
The bull-necked man and I.
Seeing you here brave and water-clean,
Leaven for the heavy ones of earth,
I am swift to feel that what makes
The plodder glad is good; and
Whatever is good is God.
The wonder is that you are here;
I have seen the queer in queer places,
But never before a heaven-fed
Naiad of the Carnival-Tank!
Little Diver, Destiny for you,
Like as for me, is shod in silence;
Years may seep into your soul
The bacilli of the usual and the expedient;
I implore Neptune to claim his child to-day!

The Wife-Woman

Maker-of-Sevens in the scheme of things
From earth to star;
Thy cycle holds whatever is fate, and
Over the border the bar.
Though rank and fierce the mariner
Sailing the seven seas,
He prays, as he holds his glass to his eyes,
Coaxing the Pleiades.

I cannot love them; and I feel your glad
Chiding from the grave,
That my all was only worth at all, what
Joy to you it gave.
These seven links the *Law* compelled
For the human chain—
I cannot love *them*; and *you*, oh,
Seven-fold months in Flanders slain!

A jungle there, a cave here, bred six
And a million years,
Sure and strong, mate for mate, such
Love as culture fears;
I gave you clear the oil and wine;
You saved me your hob and hearth—
See how *even* life may be ere the
Sickle comes and leaves a swath.

But I can wait the seven of moons,
Or years I spare,
Hoarding the heart's plenty, nor spend

A drop, nor share—
So long but outlives a smile and
A silken gown;
Then gaily I reach up from my shroud,
And you, glory-clad, reach down.

Translation

We trekked into a far country,
My friend and I.
Our deeper content was never spoken,
But each knew all the other said.
He told me how calm his soul was laid
By the lack of anvil and strife.
"The wooing kestrel," I said, "mutes his mating-note
To please the harmony of this sweet silence."
And when at the day's end
We laid tired bodies 'gainst
The loose warm sands,
And the air fleeced its particles for a coverlet;
When star after star came out
To guard their lovers in oblivion—
My soul so leapt that my evening prayer
Stole my morning song!

Dunbar

Ah, how poets sing and die!
Make one song and Heaven takes it;
Have one heart and Beauty breaks it;
Chatterton, Shelley, Keats and I—
Ah, how poets sing and die!

[Earth, I thank you]

Earth, I thank you
for the pleasure of your language
You've had a hard time
bringing it to me
from the ground
to grunt thru the noun
To all the way
feeling   seeing   smelling   touching
—awareness
I am here!

Grapes: Still-Life

Snugly you rest, sweet globes,
Aged essence of the sun;
Copper of the platter
Like that you lie upon.

Is so well your heritage
You need feel no change
From the ringlet of your stem
To this bright rim's flange;

You green-white Niagara,
Cool dull Nordic of your kind,—
Does your thick meat flinch
From these . . . touch and press your rind?

Caco, there, so close to you,
Is the beauty of the vine;
Stamen red and pistil black
Thru the curving line;

Concord, the too peaceful one
Purpling at your side,
All the colours of his flask
Holding high in pride . . .

This, too, is your heritage,
You who force the plight;
Blood and bone you turn to them
For their root is white.

Creed

If my garden oak spares one bare ledge
For boughed mistletoe to grow and wedge;
And all the wild birds this year should know
I cherish their freedom to come and go;
If a battered worthless dog, masterless, alone,
Slinks to my heels, sure of bed and bone;
And the boy just moved in, deigns a glance-assay,
Turns his pockets inside out, calls, "Come and play!"
If I should surprise in the eyes of my friend
That the deed was *my* favor he'd let me lend;
Or hear it repeated from a foe I despise,
That I whom he hated was chary of lies;
If a pilgrim stranger, fainting and poor,
Followed an urge and rapped at my door,
And my husband loves me till death puts apart,
Less as flesh unto flesh, more as heart unto heart:
I may challenge God when we meet That Day,
And He dare not be silent or send me away.

Lines to a Nasturtium

(A Lover Muses)

Flame-flower, Day-torch, Mauna Loa,
I saw a daring bee, today, pause, and soar,
    Into your flaming heart;
Then did I hear crisp, crinkled laughter
As the furies after tore him apart?
    A bird, next, small and humming,
Looked into your startled depths and fled . . .
Surely, some dread sight, and dafter
    Than human eyes as mine can see,
Set the stricken air waves drumming
    In his flight.

Day-torch, Flame-flower, cool-hot Beauty,
I cannot see, I cannot hear your flutey
Voice lure your loving swain,
But I know one other to whom you are in beauty
Born in vain:
Hair like the setting sun,
Her eyes a rising star,
Motions gracious as reeds by Babylon, bar
All your competing;
Hands like, how like, brown lilies sweet,
Cloth of gold were fair enough to touch her feet . . .
Ah, how the sense reels at my repeating,
As once in her fire-lit heart I felt the furies
Beating, beating.

White Things

Most things are colorful things—the sky, earth, and sea.
Black men are most men; but the white are free!
White things are rare things; so rare, so rare
They stole from out a silvered world—somewhere.
Finding earth-plains fair plains, save greenly grassed,
They strewed white feathers of cowardice, as they passed;
          The golden stars with lances fine,
          The hills all red and darkened pine,
They blanched with their wand of power;
And turned the blood in a ruby rose
To a poor white poppy-flower.

They pyred a race of black, black men,
And burned them to ashes white; then,
Laughing, a young one claimed a skull,
For the skull of a black is white, not dull,
          But a glistening awful thing;
          Made, it seems, for this ghoul to swing
In the face of God with all his might,
And swear by the hell that sired him:
          "Man-maker, make white!"

[God never planted a garden]

God never planted a garden
But He placed a keeper there;
And the keeper ever razed the ground
And built a city where
God cannot walk at the eve of day,
Nor take the morning air.

Life-Long, Poor Browning . . .

Life-long, poor Browning never knew Virginia,
Or he'd not grieved in Florence for April sallies
Back to English gardens after Euclid's linear:
Clipt yews, Pomander Walks, and pleachèd alleys;

Primroses, prim indeed, in quite ordered hedges,
Waterways, soberly, sedately enchanneled,
No thin riotous blade even among the sedges,
All the wild country-side tamely impaneled . . .

Dead, now, dear Browning, lives on in heaven,
(Heaven's Virginia when the year's at its Spring)
He's haunting the byways of wine-aired leaven
And throating the notes of the wildings on wing;

Here canopied reaches of dogwood and hazel,
Beech tree and redbud fine-laced in vines,
Fleet clapping rills by lush fern and basil,
Drain blue hills to lowlands scented with pines . . .

Think you he meets in this tender green sweetness
Shade that was Elizabeth . . . immortal completeness!

Questing

Let me learn now where Beauty is;
My day is spent too far toward night
To wander aimlessly and miss her place;
To grope, eyes shut, and fingers touching space.

Her maidens I have known, seen durance beside,
Handmaidens to the Queen, whose duty bids
Them lie and lure afield their Vestal's acolyte,
Lest a human shake the throne, lest a god should know his
    might:
Nereid, daughter of the Trident, steering in her shell,
Paused in voyage, smile beguiling, tempted and I fell;
Spiteful dryads, sport forsaking, tossing birchen wreathes,
Left the Druidic priests they teased so
In the oaken trees, crying, "Ho a mortal! here a believer!"
Bound me, she who held the sceptre, stricken by her, ah,
    deceiver . . .
But let me learn now where Beauty is;
I was born to know her mysteries,
And needing wisdom I must go in vain:
Being sworn bring to some hither land,
Leaf from her brow, light from her torchèd hand.

Before the Feast of Shushan

Garden of Shushan!
After Eden, all terrace, pool, and flower recollect thee:
Ye weavers in saffron and haze and Tyrian purple,
Tell yet what range in color wakes the eye;
Sorcerer, release the dreams born here when
Drowsy, shifting palm-shade enspells the brain;
And sound! ye with harp and flute ne'er essay
Before these star-noted birds escaped from paradise awhile to
Stir all dark, and dear, and passionate desire, till mine
Arms go out to be mocked by the softly kissing body of the
     wind—
Slave, send Vashti to her King!

The fiery wattles of the sun startle into flame
The marbled towers of Shushan:
So at each day's wane, two peers—the one in
Heaven, the other on earth—welcome with their
Splendor the peerless beauty of the Queen.

Cushioned at the Queen's feet and upon her knee
Finding glory for mine head,—still, nearly shamed
Am I, the King, to bend and kiss with sharp
Breath the olive-pink of sandaled toes between;
Or lift me high to the magnet of a gaze, dusky,
Like the pool when but the moon-ray strikes to its depth;
Or closer press to crush a grape 'gainst lips redder
Than the grape, a rose in the night of her hair;
Then—Sharon's Rose in my arms.

And I am hard to force the petals wide;
And you are fast to suffer and be sad.
Is any prophet come to teach a new thing
Now in a more apt time?
Have him 'maze how you say love is sacrament;

How says Vashti, love is both bread and wine;
How to the altar may not come to break and drink,
Hulky flesh nor fleshly spirit!

I, thy lord, like not manna for meat as a Judahn;
I, thy master, drink, and red wine, plenty, and when
I thirst. Eat meat, and full, when I hunger.
I, thy King, teach you and leave you, when I list.
No woman in all Persia sets out strange action
To confuse Persia's lord—
Love is but desire and thy purpose fulfillment;
I, thy King, so say!

Requiem

Oh, I who so wanted to own some earth,
Am consumed by the earth instead:
Blood into river
Bone into land
          The grave restores what finds its bed.

Oh, I who did drink of Spring's fragrant clay,
Give back its wine for other men:
Breath into air
Heart into grass
          My heart bereft—I might rest then.

Change

This day is here I hoped would come at last,
When I, a man, should live again a tree
The dregs I drained with Life in days long passed
Now thru my body courage in ecstasy
Awhile I lived apprenticed warm to flesh
And son the passioned errands of the sun:
Where lifted on the wing of some bright mesh
Of streaming wind, or dropped too deep, and spun
Into some dark abyss of circling wave,—
If so a votary come to Charybdis
With his clear torch fed from a heart—and as brave
Still now that I am such a splendid tree
There is only God and man to buffet me.
Can only those who hate you, Life, know bliss . . .

For Jim, Easter Eve

If ever a garden was a Gethsemane,
with old tombs set high against
the crumpled olive tree—and lichen,
this, my garden has been to me.
For such as I none other is so sweet:
Lacking old tombs, here stands my grief,
and certainly its ancient tree.

Peace is here and in every season
a quiet beauty.
The sky falling about me
evenly to the compass . . .
What is sorrow but tenderness now
in this earth-close frame of land and sky
falling constantly into horizons
of east and west, north and south;
what is pain but happiness here
amid these green and wordless patterns,—
indefinite texture of blade and leaf:

Beauty of an old, old tree,
last comfort in Gethsemane.

Substitution

Is Life itself but many ways of thought,
Does *thinking* furl the poets' pleiades,
Is in His slightest convolution wrought
These mantled worlds and their men-freighted seas?
He thinks—and being comes to ardent things:
The splendor of the day-spent sun, love's birth,—
Or dreams a little, while creation swings
The circle of His mind and Time's full girth . . .
As here within this noisy peopled room
My thought leans forward . . . quick! you're lifted clear
Of brick and frame to moonlit garden bloom,—
Absurdly easy, now, our walking, dear,
Talking, my leaning close to touch your face . . .
His All-Mind bids us keep this sacred place!

[Thou art come to us, O God, this year]

Thou art come to us, O God, this year—
Or how come these wisteria boughs
Dripping with the heavy honey of the Spring
Art here. For who but Thou could in living bring
This loveliness beyond all
Our words for prayer
And blur of leafish shadows, leaf in ochre,
Orchid of bloom with bright tears
Of Thy April's grief,
We thank Thee great God—
We who must now ever house
In the body-cramped places age has doomed—
That to us come Even sweet pangs
Of the Soul's illimitable sentience
Seeing the wisteria Thou has bloomed!

He Said:

"Your garden at dusk
Is the soul of love
Blurred in its beauty
And softly caressing;
I, gently daring
This sweetest confessing,
Say your garden at dusk
Is your soul, My Love."

ANGELINA WELD GRIMKÉ

Selections from Uncollected Poems

In *Aphrodite's Daughters*, a classic study of black women's poetry in the Harlem Renaissance, Maureen Honey takes note of the fact that Angelina Weld Grimké (1880–1958) "was arguably the first African American woman to publish lesbian-themed poetry." Grimké is mainly remembered today for her anti-lynching play *Rachel* (1916), but from her earliest adolescence she wrote poetry in her private notebooks, and she continued to write poetry throughout her life, though her work remained largely unpublished in her lifetime. Intensely lyrical and often erotically charged, Grimké's poems meld dashes of symbolist and early modernist imagism with strong Pre-Raphaelite tonalities and diction. In her work she assumes the reality of interracial and lesbian desire and expresses both with an undisguised ardor that was provocative and even dangerous in an era when Jim Crow segregation was at its historical peak and racial segregation not infrequently violently enforced, circumstances that likely explain her reluctance to publish. She also explores visions of sublimity or vacancy, often alluding to reserves of profound emotional despair.

Grimké was born into a family that had deep ties to the Washington, DC, black elite. Her father, Archibald Grimké, rose to become a lawyer and diplomat despite having been born into slavery in 1849 to Henry W. Grimké, the white master who owned his mother, Nancy Weston. Like his younger brother Francis James Grimké (who became one of the city's most important black religious leaders), Archibald was able to obtain education in the new freedmen's schools and universities founded after the Civil War. They were lucky to get support from the famous white abolitionist sisters Angelina and Sarah Grimké, who recognized the brothers as kin upon discovering that they were related. Archibald Grimké's marriage to Sarah Stanley, a white woman, was largely unhappy. This meant that the young poet's early life was marked by those troubles, including her mother's suicide in 1898, when Angelina was eighteen.

Her youth and education were often disrupted by her family situation. In 1895 she was abruptly taken out of the famous M Street High School in Washington, a segregated school for African Americans, and sent to Carleton Academy, a mostly white boarding school in Minnesota. After graduating and finding work as a teacher in DC—including for a time at Paul Laurence Dunbar High School—Grimké was fortunate to be able to rely on a circle of friends, most of them connected to M Street High, who were actively reshaping and contesting the race and gender lines of national life. They included the civil rights and education leader Nannie Helen Burroughs; Mary P. Burrill, a playwright and close confidante; Burrill's partner, Lucy Diggs Slowe; Coralie Franklin Cook; Mary Church Terrell; and Anna Julia Cooper—black women who were powerful activists, leaders in education, and feminist intellectuals who shared strong bonds of affection.

Despite the challenges and turbulence of her upbringing, Angelina Grimké remained very close to her father, who supported her and encouraged her to pursue her writing. His death in 1930 was especially hard for her, and in the wake of it she gave up poetry and entered a period of reclusive silence that lasted twenty-eight years, until her death in New York City in 1958. Her retirement from writing, her expressions of lesbian desire, and the fact that so much of her work remained in her private notebooks conspired to keep her from view until black feminist critics and poets began rediscovering her in the early 1980s. These qualities have kept her minor and often in the margins; those same qualities, however, are today more worthy than ever of our attention and critical engagement. It may be that the generation that can embrace Grimké and her work is only just now emerging.

Fragment

I am the woman with the black black skin
I am the laughing woman with the black black face
I am living in the cellars and in every crowded place
   I am toiling just to eat
   In the cold and in the heat
     And I laugh
I am the laughing woman who's forgotten how to weep
I am the laughing woman who's afraid to go to sleep

The Black Finger

I have just seen a most beautiful thing
        Slim and still,
      Against a gold, gold sky,
      A straight black cypress,
          Sensitive,
          Exquisite,
          A black finger
          Pointing upwards.
Why, beautiful still finger, are you black?
And why are you pointing upwards?

At April

Toss your gay heads,
    Brown girl trees;
Toss your gay lovely heads;
Shake your downy russet curls
All about your brown faces;
Stretch your brown slim bodies;
Stretch your brown slim arms;
Stretch your brown slim toes.
Who knows better than we
With the dark, dark bodies
What it means
When April comes a-laughing and a-weeping
Once again
At our hearts?

Trees

God made them very beautiful, the trees:
He spoke and gnarled of bole or silken sleek
They grew; majestic bowed or very meek;
Huge-bodied, slim; sedate and full of glees.
And He had pleasure deep in all of these.
And to them soft and little tongues to speak
Of Him to us, He gave, wherefore they seek
From dawn to dawn to bring us to our knees.

Yet here amid the wistful sounds of leaves,
A black-hued gruesome something swings and swings,
Laughter it knew and joy in little things
Till man's hate ended all. ——And so man weaves.
And God, how slow, how very slow weaves He—
Was Christ Himself not nailèd to a tree?

A Winter Twilight

A silence slipping around like death,
Yet chased by a whisper, a sigh, a breath;
One group of trees, lean, naked and cold,
Inking their crests 'gainst a sky green-gold;

One path that knows where the corn flowers were;
Lonely, apart, unyielding, one fir;
And over it softly leaning down,
One star that I loved ere the fields went brown.

Tenebris

There is a tree, by day,
That, at night,
Has a shadow,
A hand huge and black,
With fingers long and black.
    All through the dark,
Against the white man's house,
    In the little wind,
The black hand plucks and plucks
    At the bricks.
The bricks are the color of blood and very small.
    Is it a black hand,
    Or is it a shadow?

To the Dunbar High School

And she shall be the friend of youth for aye:
Of quickening youth whose eyes have seen the gleam;
Of youth between whose tears and laughter stream
Bright bows of hope; of youth, audacious, gay,
Who dares to know himself a Caesar, say,
A Shakespeare or a Galahad. The dream
To him is real; and things are as they seem,
For beauty veils from him the feet of clay.

How holy and how wonderful her trust—
Youth's friend—and, yes, how blest. For down the west
Each day shall go the sun, and time in time
Shall die, the unborn shall again be dust;
But she with youth eternal on her breast,
Immortal, too, shall sit serene, sublime.

The Eyes of My Regret

Always at dusk, the same tearless experience,
The same dragging of feet up the same well-worn path
To the same well-worn rock;
The same crimson or gold dropping away of the sun,
The same tints,—rose, saffron, violet, lavender, grey,
Meeting, mingling, mixing mistily;
Before me the same blue black cedar rising jaggedly to
      a point;
Over it, the same slow unlidding of twin stars,
Two eyes unfathomable, soul-searing,
Watching, watching, watching me;
The same two eyes that draw me forth, against my will
      dusk after dusk;
The same two eyes that keep me sitting late into the
      night, chin on knees,
Keep me there lonely, rigid, tearless, numbly miserable,
      The eyes of my Regret.

Death

When the lights blur out for thee and me,
    And the black comes in with a sweep,
I wonder—will it mean life again,
    Or sleep?

Vigil

You will come back, sometime, somehow;
But if it will be bright or black
I cannot tell; I only know
        You will come back.

Does not the spring with fragrant pack
Return unto the orchard bough?
Do not the birds retrace their track?

All things return. Some day the glow
Of quick'ning dreams will pierce your lack;
And when you know I wait as now
        You will come back.

For the Candle Light

The sky was blue, so blue that day,
  And each daisy white, so white,
O, I knew that no more could rains fall grey
  And night again be night.

I *knew*, I *knew*. Well, if night is night,
  And the grey skies greyly cry,
I have in a book for the candle light,
  A daisy dead and dry.

Grass Fingers

Touch me, touch me,
Little cool grass fingers,
Elusive, delicate grass fingers.
With your shy brushings,
Touch my face—
My naked arms—
My thighs—
My feet.
Is there nothing that is kind?
You need not fear me.
Soon I shall be too far beneath you,
For you to reach me, even,
With your tiny, timorous toes.

Greenness

Tell me is there anything lovelier,
    Anything more quieting
Than the green of little blades of grass
And the green of little leaves?

Is not each leaf a cool green hand,
Is not each blade of grass a mothering green finger,
Hushing the heart that beats and beats and beats?

Brown Girl

In the hot gold sunlight,
    Brown girl, brown girl,
        You smile;
And in your great eyes,
        Very gold, very bright,
            I see little bells,
        Shaking so lazily,
            (Oh! small they are) . . . . .
        I hear the bells.

But at fawn dusk,
    Brown girl, brown girl,
        I see no smile,
        I hear no bells.
Your great eyes
Are quiet pools;
They have been drinking, drinking,
        All the day,
The hot gold of sunlight.
Your eyes spill sunlight
        Over the dusk.
        Close your eyes,
I hear nothing but the beating of my heart.

A Mona Lisa

1

I should like to creep
Through the long brown grasses
   That are your lashes;
I should like to poise
   On the very brink
Of the leaf-brown pools
   That are your shadowed eyes;
I should like to cleave
   Without sound,
Their glimmering waters,
   Their unrippled waters,
I should like to sink down
   And down
      And down . . . . .
         And deeply drown.

2

Would I be more than a bubble breaking?
   Or an ever-widening circle
   Ceasing at the marge?
Would my white bones
   Be the only white bones
Wavering back and forth, back and forth
   In their depths?

El Beso

Twilight—and you,
Quiet—the stars;
Snare of the shine of your teeth,
Your provocative laughter,
The gloom of your hair;
Lure of you, eye and lip;
Yearning, yearning,
Languor, surrender;
    Your mouth,
And madness, madness,
Tremulous, breathless, flaming,
The space of a sigh;
Then awakening—remembrance,
Pain, regret—your sobbing;
And again quiet—the stars,
Twilight—and you.

Oh, My Heart, for the Spring!

I

Oh, my heart, for the green,—the first green!
    The shy sheen
Of the wistful sun-beams mid the gray
    Tangled sway
Of the proud, yearning arms giving birth:
    Oh, the mirth!
At the first, of the mad, moving masses
    Of grasses,
With the joy on their lips, in the clean
    Air so keen:
Oh, my heart, for the green,—the first green.

II

Oh, my heart, for the mouth,—the first mouth
    From the South!
To awake at the break of the day,
    In the gray
And the quiet and hear the first throat,
    The first note,
From the lands far away o'er the swell;
    Drink the smell
Of the jessamine bud and the rose,
    And the glows
Of the graceful fair things,—for uncouth
    Is this drouth:
Oh, my heart, for the mouth,—the first mouth.

Under the Days

The days fall upon me;
One by one, they fall,
Like leaves . . . .
They are black,
They are grey.
They are white;
They are shot through with gold and fire.
They fall,
They fall
Ceaselessly.
They cover me,
They crush,
They smother.
Who will ever find me
Under the days?

When the Green Lies over the Earth

When the green lies over the earth, my dear,
A mantle of witching grace;
When the smile and the tear of the young child year
Dimple across its face,
And then flee. When the wind all day is sweet
With the breath of growing things;
When the wooing bird lights on restless feet
And chirrups and trills and sings
        To his lady-love
        In the green above;
Then oh! my dear, when the youth's in the year,
Yours is the face that I long to have near,
        Yours is the face, my dear.

But the green is hiding your curls, my dear,
Your curls so shining and sweet;
And the gold-hearted daisies this many a year
Have bloomed and bloomed at your feet,
And the little birds just above your head
With their voices hushed, my dear,
For you have sung and have prayed and have plead
        This many, many a year.
        And the blossoms fall.
        On the garden wall,
And drift like snow on the green below.
        But the sharp thorn grows
        On the budding rose,
And my heart no more leaps at the sunset glow.
For oh! my dear, when the youth's in the year,
Yours is the face that I long to have near,
Yours is the face, my dear.

The Penguin Anthology of Twentieth-Century American Poetry

Edited by Rita Dove

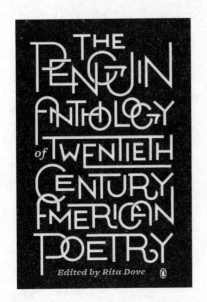

Pulitzer Prize winner and former poet laureate of the United States Rita Dove introduces readers to the most significant and compelling poems of the past hundred years. This volume represents the full spectrum of sensibilities—with varying styles, voices, themes, and cultures. Dove's selections paint a dynamic and cohesive portrait of modern American poetry.